*Another
City*

Christian Mission and Modern Culture

EDITED BY
ALAN NEELY, H. WAYNE PIPKIN,
AND WILBERT R. SHENK

In the series:

Another City

An Ecclesiological Primer
for a Post-Christian World

BARRY A. HARVEY

TRINITY PRESS INTERNATIONAL
Harrisburg, Pennsylvania

Trinity Press International, P.O. Box 1321, Harrisburg, PA 17105

Trinity Press International is a division of the Morehouse Group

Biblical quotations are from the New Revised Standard Version of the Bible, copyright 1989 by the Division of Christian Education of the National Council of the Churches of Christ in the USA. Used by permission. All rights reserved.

Cover design: Brian Preuss

Library of Congress Cataloging-in-Publication Data

Harvey, Barry, 1954-
    Another city : an ecclesiological primer for a post-Christian world / Barry A. Harvey.
        p.   cm. − (Christian mission and modern culture)
    Includes bibliographical references.
    ISBN 1-56338-277-6 (pbk. : alk. paper)
    1. Church and the world.   I. Title.   II. Series.
BR115.W6H37   1999
261′.1 − dc21   99-28179

Printed in the United States of America

99   00   01   02   03   04   10   9   8   7   6   5   4   3   2   1

Contents

97042

Preface to the Series

Both Christian mission and modern culture, widely regarded as antagonists, are in crisis. The emergence of the
modern mission movement in the early nineteenth century
cannot be understood apart from the rise of technocratic
society. Now, at the end of the twentieth century, both
modern culture and Christian mission face an uncertain
future.

One of the developments integral to modernity was the
way the role of religion in culture was redefined. Whereas
religion had played an authoritative role in the culture of
Christendom, modern culture was highly critical of religion and increasingly secular in its assumptions. A sustained
effort was made to banish religion to the backwaters of
modern culture.

The decade of the 1980s witnessed further momentous
developments on the geopolitical front with the collapse of
communism. In the aftermath of the breakup of the system of power blocs that dominated international relations
for a generation, it is clear that religion has survived even
if its institutionalization has undergone deep change and
its future forms are unclear. Secularism continues to oppose
religion, while technology has emerged as a major source
of power and authority in modern culture. Both confront
Christian faith with fundamental questions.

The purpose of this series is to probe these developments

from a variety of angles with a view to helping the church understand its missional responsibility to a culture in crisis. One important resource is the church's experience of two centuries of cross-cultural mission that has reshaped the church into a global Christian *ecumene.* The focus of our inquiry will be the church in modern culture. The series (1) examines modern/postmodern culture from a missional point of view; (2) develops the theological agenda that the church in modern culture must address in order to recover its own integrity; and (3) tests fresh conceptualizations of the nature and mission of the church as it engages modern culture. In other words, these volumes are intended to be a forum where conventional assumptions can be challenged and alternative formulations explored.

This series is a project authorized by the Institute of Mennonite Studies, research agency of the Associated Mennonite Biblical Seminary, and supported by a generous grant from the Pew Charitable Trusts.

Editorial Committee

ALAN NEELY
H. WAYNE PIPKIN
WILBERT R. SHENK

Author's Preface

Since the church's inception, says R. A. Markus, the question of what the church was has haunted Christian history. What was essential to its life and witness, and what was indifferent, "merely linked with the particular form of the society in which it was embodied"? This question has agitated Christians time and again, especially during those periods "of rapid or profound cultural change, or at moments of new encounters with foreign cultures" (Markus 1990:1). It does not take great powers of observation to realize that the church once again finds itself at just such a juncture, with both rapid, profound cultural change and new encounters with foreign cultures pressing upon it with tremendous force. Perhaps this is as it should be, for such forces constantly push the Christian community to consider anew how history unfolds according to its own practices and traditions. These ecclesial resources and insights neither seal off the body of Christ from the rest of the world nor prevent Christians from learning things about themselves and the rest of creation from those outside their fellowship. Instead, they allow the church to engage the perils and possibilities of this age in creative and redemptive ways.

I have subtitled this book "An Ecclesiological Primer for

a Post-Christian Age" because I do not attempt to put forward a comprehensive doctrine of the church in these few pages. For example, I do not consider in detail questions connected to the sacraments, polity, authority, or other related topics. These are very important matters, and no one should take their absence from this volume as an indication that I think otherwise. They are not included in part because of the limitations of the series in which the present work is published. But more to the point, I contend that we can adequately address these concerns only after the Christian community has taken up for its own time the basic question that Markus formulates so well for us. What is the church, and what is essential to it, particularly in a "post-Christian" age? Indeed, what does it mean to speak of a post-Christian age? It is only on the basis of our response to these and related matters that these other questions, as important as they are, will be properly asked and answered.

The ideas and arguments that are found in this volume have been developed in a variety of papers and articles written over the past several years. One can never adequately thank all the people whose efforts have helped to clarify what I have tried to say in these earlier works as well as in these pages. Achievements of this kind always begin with the support and love of one's family, and I am most blessed in this regard. Curtis Freeman, Stanley Hauerwas, and Scott Moore were kind enough to read the entire manuscript and made splendid suggestions at several points. John W. de Gruchy, Jean Elshtain, Wayne Whitson Floyd, Jr., L. Gregory Jones, Charles Marsh, Patricia A. Schoelles, Glen Stassen, and Ralph Wood heard or read portions of what has gone into this work and provided invaluable input. I also benefited greatly from the wisdom and encouragement of my colleagues at Baylor University. Finally, Wilbert R. Shenk, Wayne Pipkin, and Alan Neely, the editors of this series, were most generous as they guided this volume toward publication.

Introduction

The Dispersion of the Church in a Post-Christian World

Ask ten people at random what they think about the state of the world in which they live, and you will probably hear at least fifteen different opinions. Some will tell you these are the best of times, an era of unrivaled prosperity and opportunity. For others as they struggle from day to day just to survive, the times are not so good. Although the vast majority will report that they are incredibly busy as they go about their daily affairs, they will be evenly divided over the question of whether this is a good thing or not. One thing is certain, however. Few will see any viable alternative to what the world presently offers them on the horizon.

In a brief yet powerful excerpt from her novel *Jazz,* Toni Morrison puts her finger squarely on what distinguishes life in "the City," an apt figure for the world that virtually all human beings now inhabit. The narrator in the story says the following about one of the main characters:

> Take my word for it, he is bound to the track. It pulls him like a needle through the groove of a Bluebird record. Round and round about the town. That's the way the City spins you. Makes you do what it wants,

1

go where the laid-out roads say to. All the while let-
ting you think you're free; that you can jump into
thickets because you feel like it. There are no thickets here and if mowed grass is okay to walk on the
City will let you know. You can't get off the track a
City lays for you (Morrison 1993:120).

Morrison displays in splendid fashion the irony of contemporary life for all to see. The irony is deep, pervasive, and
seemingly all-encompassing. In virtually every corner of the
globe human beings spin round and round, living out their
lives as individuals paradoxically compelled in their "private" lives to make choices from a range of options that
are enumerated and managed by institutions they cannot
see and people they never meet face-to-face.[1] The kind of
robust (if frequently untidy) diversity that distinguishes a
vital social order — one in which differences are not immediately consigned to the sphere of consumer preference that
is regimented by the cultural logic of late capitalism (see
Jameson 1991) — is conspicuously absent. "Do what you
please in the City," Morrison concludes, "it is there to back
and frame you no matter what you do" (Morrison 1993:8f).

The groove of the City is decisive, making its inhabitants believe they can do what they want and get away
with it. A peculiar mix of permissiveness and supervision
thus characterizes the comings and goings of the global
Cosmopolis, as people do exactly what it wants them to
do, yet all the while saying to themselves that they are
free. This mixture drives the conformity that underlies
the celebrations of pluralism and diversity in contemporary society, resulting in what Stanley Fish calls boutique
multiculturalism, which is "the multiculturalism of ethnic
restaurants, weekend festivals, and high profile flirtations

with the other in the manner satirized by Tom Wolfe under the rubric of 'radical chic'" (1997:378)[2] What differences remain, adds George Grant, "exist only in private activities: how we eat; how we mate; how we practise ceremonies. Some like pizza, some like steaks; some like girls, some like boys; some like synagogue, some like the mass. But we all do it in churches, motels, restaurants indistinguishable from the Atlantic to the Pacific" (Grant 1969:26, as cited by Beiner 1992:23f). A dreary sameness pervades virtually every sinew of the City's body politic.

Tragically, those who make up Christ's body, the church, have not avoided these tendencies. Christians, particularly in North America, constitute for the most part a rather indistinguishable lot in the modern world, assuming along with virtually everyone else that their purpose in life is to pursue their own interests in every sphere allotted to them by the institutions of our commercial republic. A majority of those who continue to call themselves Christian "retain a vague notion of religious identity but their lives are distinctively secular, with the experience of God in worship and prayer not figuring very prominently in all that they do. Increasingly these nominal Christian . . . Americans embrace the heady hedonism and narcissism of popular culture and do not see that this contradicts biblical faith" (Guroian 1994:89). Firmly ensconced in the well-worn tracks of the City, they regard religion almost exclusively as a private and inward matter, quite often as a form of therapy designed to make their lives more fulfilling. They see little or nothing wrong in regarding the church as simply another vendor of goods and services. Like the character in Morrison's novel, the City pulls them round and round about the town like a needle through the groove of a Bluebird record. And also, like their fellow City dwellers, few see any realistic alternative to what the modern world offers them, and therein lies the beginning of our story.

We see at virtually every turn — inside the church and out — the triumph of consumerism, the demise of local associations that once bound people together in purposeful ways, the proliferation of individual rights without due regard for the goods that constitute the common welfare, and the expansion of networks of expertise organized almost exclusively around means rather than ends. In addition, seemingly intractable racial and ethnic divisions and senseless violence provide yet more evidence that the ability of the City to cope with the task of achieving and sustaining a truly human form of life is being pressed to its limits. In short, says Ronald Beiner:

> We find ourselves barbarized by an empty public culture, intimidated by colossal bureaucracies, numbed into passivity by the absence of opportunities for meaningful deliberation, inflated by absurd habits of consumption, deflated by the Leviathans that surround us, and stripped of dignity by a way of living that far exceeds a human scale. We live in societies that embark upon the grandest and most hubristic collective projects, while granting their citizens only the feeblest opportunities for an effective say over the disposal of their own destiny.

The celebration of autonomous moral agency and the ethical prerogatives of free, choice-making individuals in such a context, Beiner concludes, "is a grotesque insult" (Beiner 1992:34).

Perhaps the most damning criticism of the City comes in a moving essay written by Václav Havel during the waning years of Soviet-style communism. According to Havel, the "post-totalitarian regime" that once held Eastern Europe in its grip, far from being the antithesis of liberal democratic capitalism, was "built on foundations laid by the historical encounter between dictatorship and the consumer society." The willingness and ability of human beings to accommodate to corrupt and false systems, or as Havel puts it, to "live the lie," would not be possible without "the general unwillingness of consumption-oriented people to sacrifice some material certainties for the sake of their own spiritual and moral integrity." The attractions of mass indifference prove too powerful for most people to resist, and so they are ready to surrender what is true, good, and beautiful when faced with the trivializing temptations of modern civilization. In the end, Havel asks, "is not the greyness and emptiness of life in the post-totalitarian system only an inflated caricature of modern life in general? And do we not in fact stand ... as a kind of warning to the West, revealing to it its own latent tendencies?" (Havel 1987:54).

Some might protest that such descriptions forgo careful analysis, the detailed exploration of the complexities and subtleties that characterize life in contemporary society, in favor of simplistic bashings of modernity that serve only to foment a politics of despair.[3] And yet the signs of the times, when measured by almost any standard of evidence, would suggest that so-called Western culture is in the midst of a cycle of consumption, cynicism, and conflict that threatens to rend its social fabric. Few and far between are those who still believe that humankind is on the verge of an era where all will sit under their own vines and fruit trees with no one to frighten them, and justice and righteousness will roll down like the waters of an everflowing stream. We are adrift on a stagnant pool of isolation and avarice, antipathy and boredom, uncertainty and self-centeredness.

The deep and seemingly unshakable melancholia that holds sway over large segments of our global village has led many in popular culture as well as the academy to talk about the world entering a postmodern era. There is really no consensus about what constitutes postmodernism, save possibly for the rather trivial observation that it represents some kind of reaction to modernity (which is itself a contested term). Zygmunt Bauman may well provide us with our best handle on the ambiguous meaning of postmodernity when he states that it is

> *modernity without illusions* (the obverse of which is that modernity is postmodernity refusing to accept its own truth). The illusions in question boil down to the belief that the "messiness" of the human world is but a temporary and repairable state, sooner or later to be replaced by the orderly and systematic rule of reason. The truth in question is that the "messiness" will stay whatever we do or know, that the little orders and "systems" we carve out in the world are brittle, until-further-notice, and as arbitrary and in the end contingent as their alternatives (Bauman 1993:32f).

If Bauman is right, then the enervating relativism and romanticized nihilism that many associate with postmodern thought are nothing but the inverted image of the prodigious confidence, bordering on arrogance, that once pervaded modern life and thought. As Henry Steele Commager notes in *The Empire of Reason,* the pioneers of the modern era "recognized no bounds to their curiosity, no barriers to their thought, no limits to their activities or, for that matter, to *their authority.* They took the whole earth for *their domain* and some of them the cosmos, for they were not afraid to extend *their laws* to the universe" (Commager

1977/1982:3, my emphasis). But as this confidence continues to wane in virtually every area of human endeavor, it is
not surprising that those who had once vested their hopes
in the institutions and practices of modernity quickly come
to despair of all coherence and intelligibility, not only for
themselves, but for all forms of human existence, once their
aspirations are shown to be ill-founded.

I would be remiss at this point if I failed to acknowledge that those who served as midwives to the birth of
the postmodern City did not set out to deliver a monster.
Rather, they were the rebellious children of Christendom
who sought to realize reason's sweet dream of an earthly
paradise that would be fashioned solely by human abilities
and resources. René Descartes, whom many regard as the
leading patriarch of the modern world, gave apt expression
to the prevailing sentiment of the age when he confidently
predicted that we would eventually "make ourselves, as it
were, the masters and possessors of nature, which aim is not
only to be desired for the invention of an infinity of devices
by which we might enjoy, without any effort, the fruits of
the earth and all its commodities, but also principally for
the preservation of health" (Descartes 1968:78).

The vision of a heaven on earth set in motion a series
of events that was intended to liberate women and men
from all external constraints, but instead it cut them loose
from communal roots and traditional loyalties. In a manner that is both ironic and tragic, the pioneers of modernity
sought to uncover an understanding of the self that was
prior to and independent of the contingencies of particular times and places, which offer rich and thick contexts
for becoming and staying human, but precisely for that
reason are often messy and fraught with uncertainty and
ineluctable mystery. But what they actually bequeathed to

us was a self without substance, frantically searching for something, anything, to fill it up. Moral agency was systematically sundered from meaningful points of reference beyond individual wants and desires, and in turn the self was emptied of meaningful social content.

At the same time the sweet dream of a world built and governed solely by human capacities and insights, a world that would be unfettered by supposedly outmoded notions of divine providence and the unpredictability of fortune and fate, was turning ghoulish. Never before in human history have so many suffered and died at the hands of others. Hatred, division, violence, and oppression have multiplied throughout the world at a geometric rate that would have been unimaginable to our "unenlightened" forebears. In the words of Martin Buber, "caprice and doom, the spook of the soul and the nightmare of the world," are bound inextricably together. They "get along with each other, living next door and avoiding each other, without connection and friction, at home in meaninglessness — until in one instant eye meets eye, madly, and the confession erupts from both that they are unredeemed" (Buber 1970:108).

In short, all that the City once took for granted about the world — that it is a kind of story, with a beginning, a middle, and a conclusion, and thus humans can make real, meaningful progress in life, because there are worthwhile goals to pursue — has now been called into question. History has slipped the leash that the modern age tried to put around its neck, and now humankind is left standing, emptyhanded and dumbfounded. If we listen closely, we can even detect in protests against the dehumanizing effects of secularization and the trumpeting of traditional values "a strain of self-hatred . . . a bad faith that shows itself more the more mordant and shrill the protest, as if we have to still with the sound of our own voices the deeper doubt that there is anything genuinely and intrinsically human to be defended" (Poteat 1985:4–5). No knowledge seems to command our moral assent, no *telos* beckons us as individuals or as communities. What remains, says J. Bottum, are the ironic juxtapositions that characterize the postmodern condition: "looters with cellular telephones, Van Gogh paintings in insurance company boardrooms, crucifixes in vials of urine" (Bottum 1994:28).

As I noted previously, the telltale signs of these juxtapositions are nowhere more apparent than in the church. However, we would tell only part of the story if we simply concede that Christians are not exempt from the ironic effects of our social context. The church was for over sixteen centuries actively involved in the parturition of the postmodern setting that now threatens to overwhelm it. For most of this time the Christian community saw itself as the spiritual form of Western civilization. Rodney Clapp aptly compares this arrangement to the sponsorship of famous athletes by gym-shoe manufacturers: "Western civilization has been so powerful economically, militarily, technologically and culturally that the church, in sponsoring it, has seemed close to the center not merely of a few men's and women's lives but of history itself" (Clapp 1996a:17). In this relationship the church enjoyed enormous privileges and perks, and the "success" of Western power and prestige seemed to corroborate its claims to the truth of the gospel.

At the outset of this association, it appeared that the pagan world that had ridiculed and occasionally persecuted Christianity was now open to its mission and message. Not surprisingly, says Vigen Guroian, the church took this as an invitation "to render a 'holy service' for the world," which the church thought it could perform while remaining true to its identity as "God's eschatological vehicle of passage for this world through time into the world to come" (Guroian 1987:122). As the price for sponsoring the development of Western civilization and thereby gaining access to the seats of power, the church gave up much of its original independence as a distinct group of people that for several centuries had cultivated its own patterns of behavior and standards of judgment. For a time the return on this reinvestment of its life and mission seemed to outweigh any costs it incurred as a result of restructuring its behavior and identity to the demands of empire, kingdom, canton, province, and nation-state.

Events have since proved otherwise. The theory of dual government that prevailed in the High Middle Ages — with ecclesiastical and civil authorities jointly administering a single commonwealth, and church officials supposedly having the final say — was affirmed in word but ignored in deed. In the process the original mission of the church was seriously compromised at virtually every turn, its distinctive moral and intellectual practices subordinated to interests quite alien to its own. Moreover, as time went by and certain developments took hold (principally the rise of the modern state and the development of capitalism), the civil authorities gradually became the only legitimate political power in society. A purely "secular" society emerged for the first time in history that transferred all authority over human bodies to the state's monopoly on coercive power. What was eventually left to the "spiritual" side of society was the interior governance of the soul. The (sometimes grudging, sometimes eager) acceptance of this "division of labor" on the part of the church only reinforced the absolute political authority of the state over the burgeoning culture of commerce and consumption.

The toxic effects of Christianity's sponsorship of Western civilization adversely affected both the church and the desacralized society to which the Christian community helped give birth. In particular, the privatization and individualization of faith that resulted from this filial relationship not only meant the loss of the church's distinctive social character and mission, but it also deprived Christians of the communal means and media for nurturing the kinds of imagination and reason that a secularized society desperately needs. In addition, the disembodied and ahistorical view of the human person that resulted in part from the church's abdication from the political sphere acted as one of the solvents that gradually stripped contemporary society of the resources it needs for the cultivation of civic-minded citizenship and replaced it with an unconstrained and self-centered desire to consume (Beiner 1992:127). In short, when the church lost sight of its own *raison d'être* it unwittingly helped to institute the impoverished realm of the secular, thereby unleashing the confusion, melancholia, and enmity of the postmodern age.

We must proceed carefully from this point, for it would be easy to succumb to the cynical temptation to repudiate everything about the so-called Constantinian church as completely corrupt, and yet that would only compound the problems intrinsic to that institution with further error. Many who strongly criticize what happened following the Edict of Milan in 313 c.e. paint with such broad strokes that they obscure what is in fact good and faithful and decorous from that era. There is much from the practices and traditions that developed in later centuries that Christians in a post-Christian world can and should cherish. And as Oliver O'Donovan reminds both Christian and non-Christian, although relatively little continuity with the tradition of Christendom remains, nonetheless together we are "its *dénouement,* or perhaps its *débâcle.* It was the womb in which our late-modernity came to birth. Even our refusal of Christendom has been learned from Christendom. Its insights and errors have fashioned, sometimes by repetition and sometimes by reaction, the insights and errors which comprise the platitudes of our own era" (O'Donovan 1996:194).

In addition, the church must always be mindful of the danger of a premature triumphalism, the illusion that a community can successfully avoid the ambiguities of power and so attain in the present world a perfection that in Scripture and tradition is reserved for the age to come. Many fall prey to the "phantasy life of community," the delusional hope for "a collective life without inner or outer boundaries, without obstacles or occlusions, within and between souls and within and between cities, without the perennial work which constantly legitimates and delegitimates the transformation of power into authority of different kinds." The juxtaposition of what some regard as the realm of rational politics, and therefore of totalizing domination, with an imaginary community where all are dedicated to the ideals of difference, otherness, and toleration, "leaves the individual more not less exposed to ... unmitigated power" (Rose 1996:16, 21).

Nevertheless, as matters now stand, we must question the particular ways that the missionary vis-à-vis between church and secular society was structured during the era of Christendom for at least two reasons. First, the church no longer occupies the privileged position in the postmodern world that it held in previous generations. Indeed, its current social status more closely matches that of the early church than it does any other time and place in history.

Christendom may have given birth to the late modern or postmodern era, but its progeny seldom acknowledges this filiation or pays its parent any heed. Second, we must take advantage of hindsight and deal self-critically with the often glaring disparity between what those who were responsible for the institutions of Christendom set out to accomplish and what actually transpired. Many who seek to defend what occurred following the conversion of Constantine paint with too fine a brush, proposing hair-splitting distinctions that give us a false picture of that period in history. Some in the patristic era and even later may well have interpreted the meaning of the Christian empire as a capitulation to the throne of Christ, but in the final analysis the overall terms of surrender moved conspicuously in the other direction (O'Donovan 1996:196). To be sure, we cannot turn back the clock of history, but as Gustavo Gutiérrez says, "this must not prevent us — on the contrary, it should stimulate us — to see the meaning for us today of an honest interpretation of the events that have occurred since that time." Indeed, what is ultimately at stake "is the *intellectus fidei* — the 'intelligence' or understanding of the Christian faith" (Gutiérrez 1993:3f).

It is therefore the case that "for the foreseeable future, the real bone of contention among Christian theologians and ethicists is going to be what constitutes an appropriate ecclesiology and *modus vivendi* for the churches *after Christendom*" (Guroian 1994:3). Most would agree formally with this statement, yet propose markedly different visions for what this way of getting along is to be. One possibility is to hearken back, as John H. S. Kent puts it, "to the style of the *ancien régime* ... to a society in which the churches regarded themselves as the spiritual form of a material community" (Kent 1982:viii). This nostalgia for what once was generally takes one of two different forms. Some long to recover something of the institutional or cultural synthesis between Christianity and society that once distinguished the age of Christendom.[4] Others cede the day to the forces of secularization and so relinquish much of the specificity of the gospel. This latter group occupies itself with the difficult (some would say impossible) task of finding ways to translate the Christian hope of salvation into secular terms that are acceptable to a post-Christian culture.[5] But regardless of the varying content of their proposals, few in either camp pause to ask whether the *ancien régime* was a large part of the problem and therefore not the best paradigm for a solution.

Other Christians, understandably wary of Christendom's track record, have been tempted by the old Donatist vision of a pure church unsullied by the profane world. Like Noah's Ark, which kept its occupants safe and secure from the dangers outside, a handful of groups and individuals believe that the church must seal itself off, withdraw into a separate society where its citizens will be protected from the taint of the world (see Markus 1970:112, 122, 178). As attractive as this path might seem in the postmodern City, there are two very real problems with it — one practical, the other having to do with the church's reason for existing. As for the first, there is literally no place for the church to go to remove itself from the influence of the world. Even those within intentional Christian communities must learn to deal with the problems and possibilities posed by life in the "outside" world. But of more importance, any attempt on the part of the church to withdraw from the world would be in effect a denial of its mission. The world is the object of Christ's redemptive work, and so, although the Christian community, as Christ's body, is not identical with the world, it is called on by its Lord to live in the world, for the sake of the world.

As an alternative to the idea of the church as either a separated community or the spiritual form of an already existing social body, I would like us briefly to consider what it would mean to view the body of Christ as an *altera civitas*, another city. This way of describing the people of God is a very old idea, rooted in the Scripture and traditions of both Judaism and Christianity. Christian readers, of course, will think immediately of the *civitas peregrina* described by Augustine in *City of God*. But it is important to remember that already in the New Testament we find the political concepts of city, citizen, foreigner, and commonwealth, not to mention *koinonia* (a Greek term denoting the basic patterns of relatedness that characterized the classical *polis*) and *ekklesia* (the assembly of citizens in a city), used frequently not only to identify the community of Christ's followers, but also to challenge prevailing assumptions about the way a people should order the relations between its citizens and with those outside their community (cf. Matt. 5:14; Eph. 2:12, 19; Phil. 3:20; Heb. 11:10, 16). From the standpoint of the New Testament, the life and teaching of Jesus resulted in the advent of a social group that, as those "looking for the city that is to come" (Heb. 13:14), promoted their own laws and their own patterns of behavior, resembling nothing so much as a distinct nation, but seemingly one without its own land or ancient traditions to back up its peculiar customs (Wilken 1984:119).

But, as many scholars have pointed out in recent years, the practices and convictions that characterized early Christianity as a new and radical form of social life are unintelligible apart from a politics and a polity that were more Jewish than anything else. The church saw itself as mes-

sianic Israel covenanted with the risen Lord, marking the
continuation of the story of Abraham and Sarah's offspring
under new and distinct circumstances, namely, as those "on
whom the ends of the ages have come" (1 Cor. 10:11).
When diasporic Jews of that era attended to the crucial
matters of assimilation and identity, the classical tradition
of the *polis* provided them with their essential language for
discussing both their belonging and their distinctiveness.
According to Wayne Meeks, "Their organized *politeuma* (or
whatever their immigrants' association might be called in
a local instance) was for them an alternative city. Israel,
not Alexandria or Antioch, was their ultimate moral reference point, and Israel was both the local embodiment of
Moses' ideal *polis* and the company of God's people that
transcended local boundaries and the boundaries of time"
(Meeks 1993:44; see 1993:13).

Many readers will no doubt find these references to diasporic Judaism and the apostolic church as alternative cities
puzzling, because they draw on a conception of politics that
is part of an unknown tongue in contemporary culture. In
the "premodern" world the idea of the city did not designate
merely the physical concentration of individuals and their
dwellings in a specific locale, nor was it the earliest version
of what modern political theorists call the state. Neither
did it refer solely to what social scientists now call civil
society, the network of secondary associations — religious
bodies, fraternal organizations, trade unions, and the like —
that operate under the protection of the political umbrella
provided by the state (though the antique *polis* certainly en-
compassed these kinds of institutions). In classical Greece,
the city was the dominant form of ordered social life, and
so in the Greco-Roman world it came to signify the entire
mode of living that made for a truly human existence. The

practices and institutions of the *polis* cultivated the requisite relationships, skills, and dispositions that allowed human beings to survive and flourish.

In the sense that we will be using it in this book, a city is fundamentally "a number of people bound together by some tie of fellowship" (Augustine *City of God* 15.8). Politics is, from this standpoint, the art and science not simply of statecraft,[6] but of everything that has to do with both the actuality and the possibility of human life, which according to the Christian tradition is realized only through participation in the divine life of the triune God. It concerns itself with the vast range of goods that the members of all communities, ranging in size from the household to vast empires, pursue in common as the constitutive elements of their humanity. Personal identity and welfare are thus bound up with those of the body politic, for the citizen, the city, and the cosmos as integral aspects of an organic whole. An individual's identity is therefore never fixed, but is determined by her or his constantly changing position within the *polis*. The priorities promoted by a city articulate the order of moral goods that gives sense and purpose to its form of community, and spell out the kind of life its citizens should pursue. The retrieval of this premodern conception of politics is crucial to the possibility of faithfully recapitulating the mission and identity of the church in a post-Christian era.

Some ask whether the idea of the city in classical antiquity provides the most appropriate image for a community in diaspora. Reinhard Hütter, for example, rightly contends that "the church is not just another instantiation of the overarching genus *'polis.'* " Hütter argues that one way the church demonstrated that it was a public in its own right in distinction from the *polis* was "to draw upon the 'other' of the antique *polis,* namely the *oikos* or household. Ephesians 2:19 shows how the church can be understood as something similar to a *polis* and to an *oikos,* though not identical with either one: 'So then you are no longer strangers (*xenoi*) and aliens (*paroikoi*), but you are citizens (*sympolitai*) with the saints and also members of the household (*oikeioi*) of God' (NRSV)" (Hütter 1994:352). There is no question that Hütter makes a valid point, and yet as we have seen, the decision to use the vocabulary of the classical *polis* was made by both postbiblical Judaism and early Christianity.

The church's rationale for drawing on imagery associated with the ancient *polis* derived, it would seem, from its self-proclaimed status as a diasporic people, that is, a community specifically determined by the lack of its own place, living in cities they did not design or construct, always looking forward "to the city…whose architect and builder is God" (Heb. 11:10). We should remember that Christians could have taken refuge under a provision in Roman law that allowed for the establishment of a *cultus privatus* dedicated to the pursuit of personal piety and otherworldly salvation, but did not do so. Instead, they proclaimed allegiance to Christ as king in a manner that required its members to renounce loyalty to Caesar, and thus they intentionally confronted Roman society with a social and this-worldly alternative that incorporated elements of its host culture while remaining a distinct people. There was no doubt on the part of the empire that the Christian people constituted a subversive presence within its social order (Westerhoff 1992:280; Wright 1992b:350, 355).

Hence it is not enough to say with Hütter that the church's place in the first century was that of the *other.* By confronting Rome *with* its own terms (though not *on* its own terms [Clapp 1996a:81]), the early church specifically positioned itself as the other of Roman society, which in turn was linked typologically to all kingdoms and empires (cf. Rev. 17–18). By selecting and creatively adapting the structure of the household to articulate its own *politeia* or constitution, the church challenged both the assumptions and the normative status of antique politics. In short, the early Christian community self-consciously constituted "a maneuver 'within the enemy's field of vision'... within enemy territory" (de Certeau 1984:37). The subversive character that came with being a maneuver within enemy territory was, it would seem, both deliberate and unavoidable, because its mission inherently involved calling into question long-standing assumptions about the way a people should order the relations between its citizens and with those outside their own particular community.

What follows, therefore, should not be read as a call for the restitution of ancient Christianity, which is neither possible nor particularly desirable (I for one am not eager to face down a lion before a bloodthirsty crowd). The story of the gospel can never be repeated identically, nor should we expect it to be, for it is an ongoing drama performed by a people who live in a wide variety of times and places. As the dramatic narrative continues in and through the lives of Christians in these different contexts, it can and must be enacted differently. We must nevertheless attend with all the critical tools at our disposal to the "crucial difference (however resistant it may be to theoretical expression) between telling a story differently and telling a different story" (Lash 1986:183). The principal aim of this brief exploration in ecclesiology is to help the church speak again in a self-consciously authoritative way and thus let it reclaim itself as a distinct people who enact a different story in the midst of the world, not for its own benefit, but for the sake of the world. Such a conception of the church, I argue, will find itself in the best position to provide a critical reading of, and a distinctive and creative way of engaging, the social dispensation that characterizes a postmodern, post-Christian society. It is to this task we now turn.

1

An Outpost of Heaven:
The Early Church as *Altera Civitas*

During the first three centuries of church history, the followers of Christ constituted a minority in a world that viewed them with suspicion. The Romans widely regarded them as self-righteous and fanatical, worshipers of a capricious deity, atheists, the enemy of humankind and of a just social order. From an imperial point of view, Christians were little more than "a new and mischievous superstition" (Suetonius, *Lives of the Caesars: Nero* 16).[7] Rome classified this new movement as a political society primarily because its adherents "regarded it as fundamental that their allegiance to Christ cut across any allegiance to Caesar." As a result, says N. T. Wright, "they were seen not just as a religious grouping, but one whose religion made them a subversive presence within the wider Roman society."[8]

The Romans had good grounds for their suspicions, writes Georges Florovsky, because it was in fact the case that

Christianity entered history as a new social order, or rather a new social dimension. From the very beginning Christianity was not primarily a "doctrine," but exactly a "community." There was not only a "Message" to be proclaimed and delivered, and "Good News" to be declared. There was precisely a New Community, distinct and peculiar, in the process of growth and formation, to which members were called and recruited. Indeed, "fellowship" (*koinonia*) was the basic category of Christian existence. Primitive Christians felt themselves to be closely knit and bound together in a unity which radically transcended all human boundaries — of race, of culture, of social rank, and indeed the whole dimension of "this world."

Christians could not give their allegiance to any political entity that belonged to this world, because the church saw itself as a *polis* or commonwealth, with its own peculiar polity. Within this city all authority in heaven and on earth had been transferred to the jurisdiction of the only true King. The body of Christ was, in short, "an 'outpost of heaven' on earth" (Florovsky 1957:133f).

From the point of view of Rome, all of this could not help but appear seditious. Florovsky notes that Rome viewed itself as "*the City*, a permanent and 'eternal' City, *Urbs aeterna*, and an ultimate City also. In a sense, it claimed for itself an 'eschatological dimension.' It posed as an ultimate solution of the human problem." The empire proclaimed itself a universal commonwealth, offering to all over whom it exercised authority the only lasting and genuine peace, the *pax romana*. In short, Rome claimed to embody the final expression of "Humanity." As with every ancient society, the Roman commonwealth was in effect a politico-ecclesiastical institution that could admit no separation of competence and authority, tolerate no division of loyalty or allegiance. The empire claimed to be omnicompetent, and the allegiance of its subjects had to be complete and unconditional. "The Church was a challenge to the Empire," writes Florovsky, "and the Empire was a stumbling block for the Christians" (Florovsky 1957:135, 137).

As this confrontation clearly indicates, the early church constituted what Václav Havel calls a parallel *polis*, a distinct community that coexisted with the dominant structures of the empire (Havel 1987:101). It was this fact, says Robert Wilken, that led those who were in authority in Rome to label Christianity as a seditious and revolutionary movement: "The life and teachings of Jesus led to the formation of a new community of people called 'the church.' Christianity had begun to look like a separate people or nation, but without its own land or traditions to legitimate its unusual customs." This parallel city was suspicious precisely because "it created a social group that promoted its own laws and its own patterns of behavior" (Wilken 1984:118f). To use a colloquial expression, Christians refused to play by the rules of the (Roman) game. Instead they insisted that "all 'meaning,' every assertion about the significance of life and reality, must be judged by reference to a brief succession of contingent events in Palestine" (Williams 1990:1), a position that struck the Romans as absurd.

The first Christians consistently described themselves as citizens of an *altera civitas*, another city, with a population garnered from every tribe and language, people and nation. Aristides of Athens, writing in the first half of the second century C.E., described his fellow Christians as an *ethnos*, a nation or people, to be compared and contrasted with Babylonians, Greeks, Egyptians, and the Jews (Meeks 1993:9). The anonymous author of a letter to someone named

Diognetus reported around the same time that although Christians live in both Greek and barbarian cities,

> according as each obtained his lot, and following the local customs, both in clothing and food and in the rest of life, they show forth the wonderful and confessedly strange character of the constitution of their own commonwealth [*politeias*]. They dwell in their own fatherlands, but as if sojourners in them; they share all things as citizens, and suffer all things as strangers. Every foreign country is their fatherland, and every fatherland is a foreign country. They marry as all men, they bear children, but they do not expose their offspring. They offer free hospitality, but guard their purity. Their lot is cast "in the flesh," but they do not live "after the flesh" (*The Epistle to Diognetus* 5.4–8).

Aristides and the author of this letter were not alone in this opinion. Early Christians regularly depicted themselves as a movement of converts, persons who separated themselves from one life and society to join another. Becoming a Christian, writes Wayne Meeks, was

> something like the experience of an immigrant who leaves his or her native land and then assimilates to the culture of a new, adopted homeland. Such a transfer of allegiances and transformation of mores requires a resocialization. That is, something like the primary socialization that occurs normally in the interactions between child and family, the process in which the self receives those components of its structure and those basic values that are contributed by its

environment, is reenacted in a new context (Meeks 1993:12).

Although the church fostered its own political identity, thereby denying ultimate authority to Roman rule, it did not seek to isolate its members from the rest of the world or concern itself solely with "the welfare of those who had decided on such a course" (Havel 1987:103). On the contrary, as the letter to Diognetus suggests, it cultivated its social existence as a distinct *politeia* within and for the sake of the world. More precisely, it saw itself playing a critical role in the advent of God's messianic kingdom by embarking on a journey that would lend shape and direction to the story of creation itself. From its standpoint the course of history turns on the advent of a new mode of corporate life, with members selected from every race and tribe, a people made of all peoples. "Inasmuch as Jesus is crucified and risen," writes James McClendon, "the making of that new community on earth, one governed by 'the politics of the Lamb,' is human history's last task" (McClendon 1994:98). Rome was cast in a supporting role in this divine drama, but its claims to ultimacy for its institutions, social conventions, or political structures were rejected.

There was from the beginning, however, one major difference between the pilgrim city of Christ and all others. This parallel *polis*, unlike every other city, had no walls, for it had no territory to defend. Its assembly (*ekklesia*) of citizens was not yet gathered together in one place, but was dispersed throughout the empire and beyond, its distinctive character as a city bound together by a distinctive tie of fellowship secured "more by endurance through time than by extension through space" (Milbank 1990:403). On its temporal pilgrimage the *altera civitas* instructed its citizens not to shun the other inhabitants of the empire. Indeed, they set up housekeeping in their midst. During the course of their stay there they built houses and planted gardens, married and raised their children, and in general sought the welfare of all. Christians made use of basically the same range of goods and endured the same kinds of hardships that everyone else in the empire did.

In general, the members of this other city expected to experience these things in ways that were largely indistinguishable from those of their fellow subjects in the empire. Nevertheless, their identity as citizens of another *res publica* made them different, noticeably different, from their neighbors, for they saw themselves as constituting the mission sent to represent the interests of the one whom they worshiped as Lord and God. As the emissaries of another commonwealth, they were constantly reminded that they had no lasting home in the empire. Instead, they awaited the city that was to come, a *civitas* with lasting foundations, a *polis* designed and ruled not by other human beings, but by the one who speaks heaven and earth into being. The members of this alternative *ekklesia* were always to remember that they were foreign visitors in the imperial city, and thus they were to regard their dwellings as though they were tents, for ultimately they were pilgrims in this world, bearing witness in their bodies to another faith, another hope, another love (Augustine, *City of God* 18.54).

To be sure, the citizens of this parallel city did not believe that God's presence and activity in the world were in any way confined within or limited by their assembly. They knew that heaven was God's throne and that the earth was but a footstool for the one who calls all things into being (cf. Ps. 33:9; Isa. 66:1). Nevertheless, God had chosen them in the drama of redemption "as the ship's company

of the Spirit, and Christian community life (thus empow-
ered) [took] on a crucial role in history." The church stood
at the heart of the messianic project, for there "the Holy
Spirit [claimed] a lasting home on earth." The messianic
community, though frail and fallible, shared in the life and
activity of the triune God through its participation in the
faithfulness of Christ (Rom. 3:26; cf. 4:16), and on that
basis was sent into the world as "the Spirit's agency for the
world mission of the gospel" (McClendon 1994:433).

In short, they believed that the wisdom of God would
be made known to the rulers and authorities in the heavenly places through them and their distinctive *politeia* (Eph.
3:10). The body of Christ, not the rulers and powers of
the present age, was the primary bearer of the meaning of
history. The church was therefore neither simply the car-
rier of a message about the work of God in the world,
nor the result of that message. Rather, this new Christian
community in which the walls were broken down "not by
human idealism or democratic legalism but by the work
of Christ [was] not only a vehicle of the gospel or only a
fruit of the gospel; it [was] the good news." The church
was therefore not merely the agency or the constituency of
a mission program, the contents of which were essentially
distinct from its practices and institutions. This community
was the mission (Yoder 1994b:91).[9]

The crucial difference between the early church and the
res publica of Rome resided in their respective conceptions
of what makes the world go round, so to speak. The way
of life fostered by the empire (but also of every social order
before and since) presupposed that antagonism and conflict
are woven into the very fabric of reality. According to this
"ontology of violence" (Milbank 1990:4),[10] the beginning
and end of the cosmos reside in the chaotic oppositions

of infinity. The presumption of original violence inexorably leads to the conclusion that only by dominating both the chaos of nature and our own malevolent tendencies through the use of violence as a countermeasure can humans impose the kind of order necessary to survive and flourish in such a world. Individuals and groups are thus set against each other in order to achieve a rough balance between opposing forces within an overarching structure. Once you construe the world in this fashion, says Jean Bethke Elshtain, "The only question is who will win and who will lose; who winds up at the top of the heap; who gets sent down. . . . [I]t is difficult, if not impossible, to get away from the implication that we are in a dog-eat-dog or, if we want to be fair to dogs, a master-eat-slave-eat-master world" (Elshtain 1995a:18, 94).

For all the changes that distinguish the medieval and the modern worlds from antiquity, one thing that did not fundamentally change was the basic ontology. Both medieval feudalism and the liberal social order of modernity perpetuated the metaphysical assumptions that prevailed in the early civilizations of the Fertile Crescent, the antique Greco-Roman world, and the heroic societies of pre-Christian Europe. Closer to our own time, the leading lights of the Enlightenment also located the beginnings and ends of the cosmos in chaos and opposition. In Thomas Hobbes's influential book *Leviathan*, for example, we read that the natural condition of human existence is the *bellum omnium contra omnes*, the war of all against all. If there is to be peace, it must be wrested from the violence of nature by a single undisputed power (Hobbes 1962).[11] It is the metaphysical supposition of original violence that underwrites Hobbes's claim (exemplified in his notion of the social contract) that the state has an absolute claim to political sovereignty. Hobbes simply saw more clearly than later "liberal" thinkers that liberalism and absolutism are the twin political offspring of this ontology (Milbank 1990:13).

The supposition of original violence is not limited to modern statecraft. We find similar descriptions of how violence can be managed only by counterviolence in Freud's myth of the murder of the primal father by resentful sons, and in several of Jung's archetypal images.[12] Many of the literary theories that currently hold sway in the academy are committed to conceptions of reality in which "difference or otherness can only be regarded as fundamentally at odds with primal unity, as fundamentally adversarial or mutually destructive" (Dawson 1995:13). Economists routinely point to the antagonisms of the market as the engine that drives the production and reproduction of life. Modern sociology as well privileges this reading of the world, as seen in Max Weber's classic statement on "the specific means peculiar to" the modern state, "namely, the use of physical force." According to Weber, "the state is a relation of men dominating men, a relation supported by means of legitimate ... violence" (Weber 1965:1). Peter Berger simply reaffirms Weber's position when he contends that "violence is the ultimate foundation of any political order" (Berger 1963:69). Reinhold Niebuhr smuggles this oppositional metaphysics into Christian theology when he baldly asserts that "conflict is inevitable, and in this conflict power must be challenged by power," by which, of course, he meant the power of the state in concert with its competitive republic of commerce and consumption (Niebuhr 1932:xv).

In contrast, the early church, configured as a parallel *polis,* posited a radically different metaphysics that denied ontological necessity to coercive rule and the antagonistic positioning of difference. This nomadic people did not regard peace as the reduction and mastery of chaos. The world instead originated through peaceful donation, the infinite unfolding of created difference as the manifold inventions of charity. Violence and opposition intruded through willful disobedience upon the original harmony of infinite charity that will nonetheless prevail in the end. They also believed that the church as *altera civitas* played an important role in the restoration and re-creation of this original harmony. Through its practices of hospitality, forbearance, forgiveness, and reconciliation, it participated in the messianic suffering of God that communicated to the world the idiom or *logos* of its beginning and end in peace (see Milbank 1990:389–432). Contrary to the caricatures that prevail in much of contemporary theology, the communal form of life fostered by the early church as *altera civitas* did not seek to withdraw from the world, but encountered head-on its most pervasive (i.e., violent) tendencies.

At this point some may be tempted to say that all this is well and good, but what does it have to do with life in a postmodern age? In our own place and time, as the world steps across the dual threshold of a new millennium and a new era, Christians once again find themselves a minority in a postmodern global village that no longer feigns loyalty to the God of Abraham and Sarah. In setting after setting the church is no longer wanted, no longer needed, or both. Many Christians are unsure on their part whether they have anything distinctive to offer either as individuals or as a community, much less give good reasons why the church should continue to exist. And so in many ways it is once again not a matter of the church's purity, but its survival and integrity that are at stake.

Given the similarity of their situation with that of the early church, we might reasonably conclude that Christians are once again cultivating patterns of conduct and reasoning analogous to those fostered by their forebears. And we would be seriously in error. Instead, the body of Christ, with precious few exceptions, continues to yearn nostalgically for the *modus vivendi* that characterized the sixteen centuries of Christendom, during which time the church not only learned to play by the rules, but helped to draft and then enforce them. This very peculiar response to a similar set of circumstances can only be explained with reference to historical changes that significantly altered how the church understood itself and its relationship to the world.

But if we are to make sense of the changes that took place over several centuries, we must first consider in more detail the distinctive character of the early Christian community. The corporate life of the first Christians is normative for later generations not simply because it was the early church, but rather because what they believed and practiced is true (Hauerwas 1988:189 n. 34). The apostolic church's consistent description of itself as an eschatological fellowship provides us with our first and most important clue to our quest. The first generations of believers saw themselves as "the people of the 'Age to Come,'" the people who are under a new covenant and hold membership in the true Israel.... [S]o marked is the proleptic sense of reality in the New Testament that the 'inheritance of Christ' is viewed not only as a transforming membership in a brotherhood which is to be but also as the fruit and function of the Spirit's operation here and now" (Lehmann 1963:14, 45–46). We must therefore examine in more detail what it meant for Christians prior to the time of Constantine to regard themselves as the people of the age to come.

2

The City That Is to Come: The Polity and Politics of the Pre-Constantinian Church

The self-understanding of the early church was by no means uniform, as evidenced by the diversity in the New Testament itself. Nevertheless, a distinctive type of narrative eschatology, "consistent in its broad outline though wondrously variable in detail" (Meeks 1993:189), figured prominently in virtually all it said and did. The first-century church professed and proclaimed what happened when the kingdom of God drew decisively near in the life, work, and death of Jesus. In particular, the first Christians noted the conflict of the kingdom with the established authorities and powers, culminating in Jesus' passion, and its vindication in his resurrection. With the ascension of the risen Christ to the right hand of God, they declared that the world was no longer the same, that it had definitively crossed the threshold of a new age. The social ties that bound them together in a new style of communal life were a definitive sign to the world that a new creation had dawned.

Nevertheless, although the triumph of God over death

signaled that this new era was at hand, Jesus' followers also realized after a time that the "end" was not yet. Indeed, in almost every way things went on as before. Babies were born, goods were bought and sold, the priests and scribes continued to gather at the Temple, the Romans looked to expand their empire further, and death still exercised its terrible authority over the created order. The early Christians struggled to find appropriate ways to describe the new situation that was taking shape in the midst of the old. They gradually came to see themselves as living in a period of time in which two ages and two social orders overlapped. There was the present age over which the authorities and powers exercise dominion, but which was passing away, and the age of God's everlasting reign, definitively inaugurated by the work of Jesus and creatively extended to the ends of the earth through the church's fellowship in the power of the Spirit. The rulers of this present age, although not directly acknowledging Christ's Lordship, had been decisively defeated and brought under his sovereignty, and thus they were the unwitting servants of God's final (though still future) triumph (cf. O'Donovan 1996:120–57, 211f; Markus 1990:87f; Wright 1997:441–74, 592–611; and Yoder 1984:136).

Through its confession of Christ's Lordship — celebrated in its eucharistic gatherings and lived out daily in a holy life of service and fellowship — the early church announced to the world that the end toward which history was moving was not determined by those whom this age calls powerful, but by the one who gathers together all things in heaven and on earth in the crucified Messiah of Israel (Eph. 1:10). The messianic rule of God established the goal toward which all things tend, and it also set the limits for the exercise of power by all worldly authorities. In and through this small group of people, everything in the created order, all life, was "now, at once, immediately confronted with a claim that is non-negotiable in the sense that in the end God will irrefutably be — God" (McClendon 1994:66).

As Georges Florovsky reminded us in the previous chapter, we would fail to grasp the meaning of the vivid and often esoteric imagery of biblical eschatology if we were to treat it as abstract components in a freestanding religious worldview. Those who reduce Christianity in this manner usually do so in order that it might be rationally compared to alternative worldviews without requiring commitment to any particular way of life or community. But these images finally make sense only "within the complex history of conflict and clarification which is the history of the Jewish and Christian people." They did not appear out of nowhere but "were usually produced in criticism of inhuman (and hence 'ungodly') practices." As a result, "it is only through the redemptive transformation of our human practices that we can acquire some sense of what the truth of these images might be when used as metaphors for our relation to . . . God" (Lash 1988:276).[13] In short, these metaphorical images are meaningful only as an integral part of a distinctive social project that is the church. Eschatological discourse is indelibly inscribed in this community's narrative interpretation of the world, and is therefore inextricably bound up together with its distinctive manner of responding to the opportunities and vicissitudes of everyday life.[14]

The eschatological ecclesiology (or ecclesial eschatology) of early Christianity did not originate with Jesus or the Twelve, nor were the people of God first constituted as another city with the coming of the Spirit on the day of Pentecost, although these certainly represent watershed

events in this story. The early Christian community saw itself rather as "the first-fruits of restored Israel and...heir
of all those confessions by which Israel had classically defined itself." To be sure, the self-portrait of the first-century
church as "messianic Israel covenanted with her risen Lord,
already the beneficiary of what the community conceived
as messianic blessings" (Meyer 1986:43), was initiated and
informed by the earthly mission of Jesus. But if the Synop-
tic Gospels are to be trusted,[15] Jesus viewed that mission as
a creative recapitulation of the history of his people. The
early church in turn saw itself, following the death and
resurrection of the servant-messiah, as "continuing Israel's
story under new circumstances" (Clapp 1996a:88).

We dare not overlook, therefore, the Jewish antecedents
to the identity of Jesus and the church. The changes that
took place during the first few centuries of the church constituted at their core a movement *away* from the origins of
the gospel in the fertile and complex state of affairs that was
first-century Judaism. We must therefore trace the origins
of early Christianity's eschatological politics through the
offspring of Abraham and Sarah, a people through whom
God would bless "all the families of the earth" by serving as
"a priestly kingdom and a holy nation" (Gen. 12:3; Exod.
19:6). The activities and institutions that set the church
apart as a radical and subversive form of life in the Roman Empire are largely unintelligible if considered apart
from a polity and politics that were thoroughly Jewish from
beginning to end.

The Rule of God in the People of Israel

The ecclesial eschatology of first-century Christianity
marked the continuation (and in a very real sense the cul-

mination) of a social drama that a relatively obscure and loosely organized group of people called Israel had enacted over a period of fifteen centuries. The main plot of this dramatic narrative is set forth in exemplary fashion in the story of Gideon, an early charismatic figure who led a small band of warriors to victory against one of their perennial enemies, the Midianites. Whereas Gideon attributed his success to the activity of the LORD, tribal elders, impressed with his courage and ingenuity, saw him as someone who could provide stability and security to a loose-knit collection of tribes struggling to survive in a harsh and unforgiving land. And so, in keeping with the practice of the nations and peoples around them, the "men of Israel" offered him the opportunity to establish a dynastic monarchy for himself and his sons. But Gideon vigorously declined their invitation, declaring instead that neither he nor his sons, but only the LORD, would rule over Israel (Judg. 6:11–8:23).

In the words of Martin Buber, what we encounter in the story of Gideon is a *poetizing memory* that expresses a will or disposition "of a religious and political kind in one." More concretely, the narrative posits "the realization of the all-embracing rulership of God" as "the beginning and end (*das Proton und Eschaton*) of the people of Israel." The desire and striving to see the reign of God become a reality functions as "an original constant in the dynamic of this folk life," educating countless generations to "know history as the dialectic of an asking divinity and an answer-refusing, but nevertheless an answer-attempting humanity." Israel's religious-political desire for the fulfillment of the divine kingship, "wresting ever and again from the changing resistance of the times a fragment of realization, however altered," formed the basis for their understanding of God, the natural world, history, and politics (Buber 1967:58, 63–65, 139).[16]

Both the form and content of Israel's narrative herme-neutics are tied to the nature of human consciousness as "that act of attention to something under the auspices of its sign." Because it is "an act which is social in its origin," and thus inseparable from the "transaction of signs with other selves" (Peray 1983:105, 87), consciousness (from the Latin *con-scio,* to know with) resides principally in the ability to hear and speak rather than in the power to see (see Hauer-was and Burrell 1977:85). This ability to say, and more precisely to signify, emanates from the contingent opera-tions of memory that form the medium and the means of human knowledge. A thing or person exists for another, or an event happens to somebody, only when it passes into an "incorporeal" or intentional state that abides through time when it no longer is present, much like the grin of the Cheshire cat in *Alice in Wonderland* (see Milbank 1990:426f). With respect to the understanding of history, memory testifies above all else that "the present situation has a context; it ... is part of a continuity, it is 'made' and so it is not immutable" (Williams 1984:29f).

The children of Abraham and Sarah learned from their communal memory that the episodes that comprise his-tory do not form a series of randomly ordered "facts."[17] The meaning of any event is never self-evident, but is in-trinsically related to what happened before it occurred, to whatever else was happening as it occurred, to what subse-quently ensued, and (perhaps of most importance) to what will happen in the future. In short, the stuff of history re-quires for its sense and significance the kind of context only memory can provide. The memory of God as king, exem-plified in the canonical story of Gideon, is therefore poetic in the basic sense of that term, for it has provided countless generations with their knowledge of how to go on and go further in the use of the expressions of a language. As a community that gradually became skilled in the use of this language and its networks of signification, Israel has known (albeit imperfectly) how to go on and further as a people who had a context and were therefore part of a continuity that was made and not immutable (MacIntyre 1988:382).[18] The biblical narrative of God as king formed the "poetizing" medium by which reason could become practical as freedom (Metz 1980:195–97).

Israel's unfolding sense of who they were and what was at stake for them as a people has thus been tied up with their sense of history "as the dialectic of an asking divinity and an answer-refusing, but nevertheless an answer-attempting humanity." The key feature in this dialectic is its interlocutory character. Over and over again the word of the LORD comes to claim this people in the entirety of their existence, and their world is turned upside down. God addresses Abraham, calling upon him to give up everything that was safe and familiar and go with his family to a land he had never seen. God addresses Moses, telling him to leave the safety of those with whom he had taken refuge and return to Egypt where his people were oppressed. God addresses David, reminding him that he was but the servant of the LORD. God addresses Elijah, assuring him that there were others who had not bowed down to idols. God addresses the author of the book of Daniel, allowing him to see in dim figures the ultimate fate that awaited the holy ones of the Most High. And at each step along the way the question of what it meant to be claimed as God's "treasured possession out of all the peoples . . . a priestly kingdom and a holy nation" (Exod. 19:5–6) is posed anew.

The interlocutory dialogue between God and the people of Israel is similar to the interpellative process that shapes the formation and transformation of self-identity. For example, Elshtain notes that the moving story of Augustine in *The Confessions* is that "of a man 'becoming a question to himself' and struggling with the immediacy of desire" (Elshtain 1995a:10). Augustine's sense of who he was, together with his desire for and understanding of the God who created and redeemed him, were painstakingly fashioned by this interpellative process. But *The Confessions* also remind us that the questions of personal identity — Who am I? What sort of person am I to become? How should I relate to others? What is my role in this place and time? — are never posed apart from some kind of social context. Each and every person becomes a self only in dialogue with others.

All of us are constantly (though most of the time implicitly) defining and redefining our identity in terms of an answer to the question, Who am I? And this question "finds its original sense in the interchange of speakers. I define who I am by defining where I speak from, in the family tree, in social space, in the geography of social statuses and functions, in my intimate relations to the ones I love, and also crucially in the space of moral and spiritual orientation within which my most important defining relations are lived out." These defining relations are themselves the product of our initiation into a language, the transaction of signs with other selves. Each of us exists as human only within the webs of interlocution formed by these transactions. We acquire our languages of moral and spiritual discernment "by being brought into an ongoing conversation by those who bring us up" (Taylor 1989:35f). Our identity as individual persons is inseparable from the reciprocal structures of accountability that are located in a community and its complex network of practices and institutions.

A similar process of interlocution is involved in determining the identity of a whole community. As we have already seen, the story of Israel is that of a people becoming a question to themselves time and again, constantly struggling with the mystery of having been chosen to be God's people. Even Israel's name testifies to the centrality of this interlocutory setting. We read in Scripture the story of Jacob wrestling all night with a mysterious figure who bears a blessing from God. Jacob, though he had been wounded by his opponent, refuses to let him go without first receiving that blessing. The stranger bestows on Jacob a new name, Israel, for "you have striven with God and with humans, and have prevailed" (Gen. 32:28). The eponym Israel, "he who strives with God," thus foreshadows the destiny that awaits this community on their pilgrimage through history.

As the story of Israel-qua-Jacob suggests, for a person (or group) to be initiated into personhood (or peoplehood) as a character in an ongoing drama does not necessarily condemn anyone to a fixed place or role within the story. It is of course the case that at any given moment in this narrative a person could be asked to provide "a certain kind of account of what one did or what happened to one or what one witnessed at any earlier point in one's life than the time at which the question is posed." But he or she may also ask others to provide some kind of account, thus putting them to the question (MacIntyre 1984:217f). Through this kind of interpellative give-and-take human beings develop innovative ways of construing who they are and what matters in their lives. But these innovations are achieved only on the basis of previously established networks and relationships. The dialectic of memory and identity continually unfolds like the contrapuntal development of a musical theme by a jazz ensemble, through the tensions and dissonances created, sustained and resolved (at least provisionally) between those who both comprise and are constituted by that group.

The webs of interlocution cultivated by a community over time create the basis for its continuing response to an implicit set of questions: Who are we, and what kind of world do we inhabit? What sort of people are we to become, and what role do we play in this world? What goods should we pursue as a people? What means should we use to achieve these goods? These questions, in turn, find sense and significance in interaction with other groups and their patterns of conduct, that is to say, in affirmation and criticism of their practices. For example, rather than personifying nature (including human nature and history) as deities, in the style of their neighbors in Mesopotamia, Egypt, and Canaan, Israel's primal relationship to the world around them took the form of response to a personal address. Persons, things, and events were interpreted as visible signs of God's activity, created and ordered by the divine utterance (see Milbank 1997b:106). Everything that occurred in heaven and on earth was thus interpreted under the sign of a text whose author was finally none other than God.

Finally, the question of what is the good and the best for one group of people invariably leads some within that group to inquire about what is the good and the best for all people. The prophets of Israel were at the forefront of this endeavor, frequently linking the identity and mission of the chosen people to the welfare of all the nations. The anonymous prophet whose words are recounted in the Book of Isaiah thus asserted that the servant of the LORD would be sent "as a light to the nations, that [God's] salvation may reach to the end of the earth" (Isa. 49:6). The systematic asking of these questions and the ongoing attempts to answer them in deed as well as in word provide creaturely life with its narrative coherence or unity. From the standpoint of Israel's canonical memory, therefore, any attempt to specify the transcendental conditions for the meaning of human actions and affections must at some point come to terms with "the inevitability of historiography" (Milbank 1990:71).

Gideon's declaration that neither he nor his offspring would occupy the throne reserved for God represents an early form of the poetizing historiography of Israel that is undoubtedly naive and nonreflecting. Nevertheless, its basic themes are integral to the increasingly complex developments in the plot of the biblical story. To change the metaphor, the ideas associated with the kingship of God in this story set forth the *cantus firmus* of Israel from its inception. They provide the primary motif around which the contrapuntal themes of law and prophecy, psalmody and wisdom, exile and apocalyptic have orchestrated the life and history of this people over the centuries. The assertion of divine rule that is at the heart of this story has forever marked Israel as an "odd people" who speak with an ultimately subversive voice (Brueggemann 1991:50–52).

The historical counterpoint of an asking divinity and an answer-attempting humanity that stands at the beginning and end of Israel's life and mission so radically calls into question the dominant categories and relations not only of Gideon's day, but of every time and place, that the restructuring of language and life continues to the present. It is indeed an audacious claim, that every assertion about the meaning of life and reality must ultimately be judged by reference to one seemingly insignificant group of people who have labored through the centuries as the (often reluctant) bearers of this poetizing memory. And yet the mission of Israel to the other nations has been (and remains so in both the Jewish and Christian communities) to allow the irreducible historicity and "intractable strangeness" (Williams 1990:1) of its originating memory to time and again challenge prevailing assumptions about how people should relate to each other, to the world in which they live, and to the one who calls that world into being.

The poetizing memory inscribed for us in the pages of Scripture does not claim Israel only at the sublime boundaries of life, that point where, as Dietrich Bonhoeffer puts it, human knowledge is said to give out ("perhaps they are just too lazy to think"), or where human resources supposedly fail. Modern institutions would confine it there as a strictly "religious" matter, but God always claims the lives of the chosen people, "not at the boundaries where human powers give out, but in the middle of the village" (Bonhoeffer 1971:281f). The tales of exodus and conquest, kings and prophets, exile and diaspora, when taken together with the praises and laments of the Psalter and the requirements of law and cult, focus the attention of the hearer squarely on the quotidian existence of this people as they struggle to survive and prosper, frequently in harsh and unforgiving circumstances.

The reign of Israel's God thus intrudes into the events that take place in the midst of everyday life, but in a way substantially different from that found in other societies. The sagas and legends of antiquity are replete with tales of how conflict between powerful forces (e.g., gods, heroes, giants) not only brings the world into existence, but also imposes order on the contingent happenings of history. In the *Enuma Elish,* a creation myth from ancient Mesopotamia, one of the formative cradles of civilization, we read that the cosmos was formed by the god Marduk from the shattered body of Tiamat, the goddess of the saltwater ocean, whom he had conquered in battle (see Pritchard 1969:60–72).[19] The Greeks — as seen in the mythology of Hesiod, the epics of Homer, the tragedies of Sophocles and Euripedes, and the studied philosophical discourse of Plato and Aristotle — likewise considered war the natural state of humankind and the material principle that bound together the *polis* (see Elshtain 1987:47–56). Within Roman mythology and politics "the principle of a prior violence 'stayed' and limited by a single violent hand" was also firmly enshrined. Romulus, the founder of the city, murdered his brother (and rival) Remus and then enslaved those whom he protected against foreign enemies. And when he went into battle, he "invoked the staying hand of Jupiter, who then received the title *stator*. The supreme God, therefore, like the founding hero, arises merely as the limiter of a preceding disorder" (Milbank 1990:391).[20] The only thing that is not arbitrary in the world thusly depicted is the ontological primacy of violence, the permanent regulation and confinement of power with power.

The selection of Israel as God's chosen people, on the other hand, was the first concrete historical sign of the original harmony that characterized creation at the outset, and into which violence intrudes only secondarily. Violence and coercion are not constitutive elements of the kingship of God as they are with all other forms of sovereignty. On the contrary, the reign of Israel's God shapes the course of history in the form of what first seems like a paradox. The divine reign manifests itself time and again through the refusal of all limits, that impulse of human beings which (to use an equestrian metaphor) constantly "refuses the bit."[21] In the case of Israel, however, this ceaseless striving to be

independent of others was not for the sake of either individual autonomy or ethnic purity, but was commissioned
and carried out for the sake of the highest bondage, for
the sake of serving the ruler of the universe. The extent of
this paradox, says Buber, is seen in the fact that this highest
bondage knows no compulsion. God has always vested this
liberating servitude in the faithfulness of those who are so
bound. Those who hear and respond in faithful obedience
can either strive toward a perfected community in freedom
or, under the auspices of divine authority, slide into some
form of anarchy (Buber 1967:138).[22]

The paradox of God's sovereign rule finds its historical
expression as a *politeia* in the covenant concluded at Sinai
between Israel and the God of their ancestors, who would
forever be their king ruling over a kingdom (*malkuth*) unlike that of any earthly king (Exod. 19:6). As soon as God
engages the people of Israel in the covenant relationship,
"the kingship of God as such emerges. It dares to embody
historically a tendency toward actualization which can be no
other than a political one. When the divine kingship brings
its unconditioned claim against the entire existence of the
people, the answer can come only from the entire existence
of the people." The Sinai covenant is thus "the first step"
on a historical pilgrimage that unfolds, for Israel as a whole
and for the individuals who are its members, "in the real
relationship . . . to a world which does not want to be God's
and to a God who does not want to compel the world to
become His" (Buber 1967:118, 139).[23]

The covenant ceremony in the wilderness of Sinai is
therefore more than a mere "spin-off" of the Exodus story,
as one noted Old Testament scholar unfortunately puts it
(Brueggemann 1991:51). No story is repeated in a social or
historical vacuum, especially one that claims to be about a

comprehensive truth that ultimately (though frequently indirectly) affects the whole of creation. Such tales have their enduring sense and significance only in a historical community that embodies a continuing narrative relation to the "original" story. Consequently, although the image of the kingship of God does not by itself specifically *denote* a particular political commonwealth, it does *connote* a distinctive form of politics. Put otherwise, the idea of divine kingship presupposes the actual formation of a people through whom the world is confronted by God's exclusive claim upon it (Wright 1992b:307).

The paradox of God's kingship thus engages the figures and events of history through a community that continuously and creatively reenacts the poetizing drama of divine sovereignty. The people of Israel — in their actions and relationships, their memories and expectations, their achievements and failures — constitute both the enduring form and content of this story. As a result, although the events of the Exodus took place before the assembly was convened at Sinai, they derive their lasting significance from what subsequently took place in the wilderness. Israel's liberation from Egypt is "*from* bondage and *for* covenant, and *what for* matters more than *what from*." Stated differently, "liberation has its postrequisites as well as its prerequisites. It is not a once-and-for-all revolution but only a threshold linking two phases of pilgrim peoplehood" (Yoder 1989:81).

The impetus generated by Israel's deliverance from Egypt thus comes to fruition only in the making of the covenant at Sinai, in the constitution of a people under the kingship of God and governed according to Torah, a term that denotes first of all not the specific list of commandments and ordinances in the Pentateuch but the story of God's election and education of a people (see Hays 1989:53). Torah was therefore holy, a constant and everlasting reminder of the exclusive and unconditional claim on them, even as they were unsure of what demands God would impose upon them in the ever-changing circumstances of history. But as important as the Sinai covenant was for Israel, providing them with their initial conception of what the LORD expected of them, it was strictly the point of departure for their historic journey. Buber states that "the striving to have the entirety of its life constructed out of its relation to the divine can be actualized by a people in no other way than that, while it opens its political being and doing to the influence of this relationship, it thus does not fundamentally mark the limits of this influence in advance, but only in the course of realization experiences or rather endures these limits again and again" (Buber 1967:118f). As the people left the wilderness of Sinai, their understanding of God's purpose in choosing them above all other nations would be both tested and transformed along the way.

The "theocracy" denoted by this complex tradition of God's kingship does not refer to an accomplished fact, that is, an institutionalized form of government. This would confuse the depiction of divine rule set forth in Scripture with hierocracy, with the rule of consecrated elites, such as a priestly cast, a monarchy sanctioned by priestly oracle, or even a deified king. Such arrangements are the antithesis of Israel's understanding of the kingship of God. Neither does theocracy denote an "ideal" or regulative concept, as it has been routinely construed by liberal Protestant theology over the course of two centuries.[24] Rather, the divine rule set forth in Israel's poetizing memory comes to expression in this people's communal will toward constitution, their desire for actualization. The theocratic disposition is neither nostalgic sentiment nor utopian fantasy but rather "the real, struggling, religious-political will to fulfillment, wresting ever and again from the changing resistance of the times a fragment of realization, however altered" (Buber 1967:59, 64).

The people of Israel thus know history, or more accurately, *re-member* history, as an interpellative dialogue between God (whose covenant faithfulness, *tsedaqah*, or "righteousness," is perpetually at stake) and humankind (whose resistance to the divine rule forms an essential component of the engine that drives history toward its true end). Those who in this exchange "represent the case for divine rulership against that of 'history,' experience therein the first shudder of eschatology." Like the physical jolt that occurs when two gigantic tectonic plates collide underneath the surface of the earth, the tug-of-war between God and humankind set off seismic tremors of a peculiar sort. As Israel embarked on "the path through the dark ravine between actualization and contradiction," they repeatedly encountered the insistent demand for an *eschaton*, when every knee would bow and every tongue confess. The eschatological trajectory that would eventually distinguish the polity and politics of the first-century church arises out of this tension between the perfection of Israel's ascribing to God exclusive sovereignty over creation and the actual state of affairs in the world (Buber 1967:64, 110, 139).

Tremors of Eschatology in the History of Israel

As Israel continued to wrestle with God and other peoples, its understanding of the divine kingship was extended and refined. Eschatological tremors continued to rumble as they established themselves in the land of Canaan. These tremors intensified in the conflict between those who sought to unify the tribes of the LORD under "a king to govern us, like other nations" (1 Sam. 8:5) and those who continued to champion the prerogatives of the divine rule. The institution of the monarchy eventually became firmly entrenched in Israel, but the kings failed for the most part to honor or even heed their designation as servants of the LORD (2 Sam. 7:19ff; 23:1–7). Although the monarchy was ultimately a failure as a political institution, it nonetheless played a crucial role in the historical development of Israel's continuing drama and figured prominently (though in unexpected ways) in the discourse of the early Christian movement.

The prophets played a key role during this period as the advocates and interpreters of God's sovereignty over against the pretensions of the royal and priestly families in the kingdoms of Israel and Judah. Contrary to popular opinion, these prophetic figures were not solitary religious geniuses who under the mysterious influence of some kind of ecstatic charisma set themselves over against the institutionalized power of canonical texts, dogmatic traditions, priestly hierarchies, and rote liturgies. Rather, they kept alive in Israel the poetizing memory of divine kingship in a variety of ways, while at the same time transforming their conception of the God they served and of themselves as the chosen people. "Thus says the LORD," they repeated over and again, preserving and promulgating the story of Israel's only true sovereign, who demanded justice from those in power, took the side of the poor and oppressed, and invited all who would listen to strive toward that future country where "they shall all sit under their own vines and under their own fig trees, and no one shall make them

afraid; for the mouth of the LORD of hosts has spoken"
(Mic. 4:4).

These tremors grew in intensity through the crisis of
the Babylonian Exile and into the ensuing period, as witnessed in the practices, institutions, and texts that developed within postexilic Judaism. It would be difficult to
overstate the significance of the Exile for the surviving
people of Israel. Even for those who had returned to the
land in the days of Cyrus of Persia, the Jews continued to
languish under the oppressive rule of foreign powers that
represented for them the exile of slavery. Their God had
not yet returned triumphantly to Zion to redeem Israel as
promised by the prophets (Isa. 52:7–10; Ezek. 43:1–9). Instead, they saw themselves as "slaves in the land that [God]
gave to our ancestors to enjoy its fruit and its good gifts.
Its rich yield goes to the kings whom [God has] set over
us because of our sins; they have power also over our bodies and over our livestock at their pleasure, and we are in
great distress" (Neh. 9:36–37). Many years before, Jeremiah
had written the exiles at the beginning of their enforced
sojourn in Babylon to tell them that they must learn to
make do in their new social circumstances and to pray for
the welfare (*shalom*) of Babylon, for their own welfare de-
pended upon that city. Only after seventy years had passed
would the Lord visit the people (Jer. 29:1–14). The reinter-
pretation of that text by the Maccabean author of Daniel
reinforced the pervasive sense that the Exile had not ended
in the sixth century B.C.E. but continued right through the
time of the great empires (see O'Donovan 1996:82–88; and
Wright 1992b:268–79 and 1997:576f).

It was in the context of the continuing exile that the unsettling queries of Ecclesiastes and Job brought into sharp
relief the eschatological tension that marked Israel's loca-

tion between their worship of God as the Lord of all reality, with no partners and no rivals, and the violent nature of life as it actually unfolds in history, or more precisely, *as* history. Far from trying to relieve or resolve the tension, these texts dealt openly with its implications for the continuing existence of the Jewish people. In the words of Qoheleth, God appoints a time for everything, and yet human beings, those creatures uniquely endowed with a sense of past and future, "cannot find out what God has done from the beginning to the end" (Eccles. 3:11).[25] More than anything else, these texts emphasized that any attempt at premature resolution of this tension would in effect be a denial of the distinctive vocation of this people.

The shockwaves of Israel's exilic eschatology once again increased in both intensity and frequency in the apocalyptic sections of the Old Testament. Anonymous authors extended and radicalized the prophetic oracles of judgment and redemption that gave direction and content to God's exercise of divine kingship. The whole cosmos, not just the people of Israel, now stood beneath God's sovereign gaze. In the modern world, the apocalyptic passages in Scripture have long been regarded as one of its most embarrassing aspects. What strikes our ears as fantastic depictions of cataclysmic upheavals and idyllic visions of an otherworldly paradise seem remote from, and ill-suited for, the kind of life demanded by contemporary lifestyles and social structures. What people require today, we are repeatedly told, are ideas and institutions that promote understanding and mutual tolerance, not wild speculations about the ends of the age, the judgment of the wicked, and the like. (One strongly suspects that class distinctions underwrite much of the distaste for apocalyptic imagery, recalling for the upwardly mobile uncomfortable memories of the rural churches and hellfire-and-damnation preaching that they have tried to leave behind.)

The modern aversion to apocalyptic eschatology, especially for its supposedly otherworldly character, may largely be attributed to the widespread but erroneous assumption that many Jews in the years leading up to the first century C.E. expected the imminent collapse of the domain of time and space, and with it all sense of history. This misguided impression is due in part to the inherent ambiguity in the word "end," which can signify either a termination of some kind or the goal of an act, and often it can refer to both. In apocalyptic discourse that speaks of "the ends of the ages" (1 Cor. 10:11), the relationship between purpose and finality is absolutely crucial, and to miss it is to miss the whole point of eschatology.[26] The ends signified in Scripture speak both of the aim and the limits of life, the course that creation is taking in history, and the consummation that awaits it. The ends of the ages mark that toward which everything tends, giving shape and direction to history, indeed, marking the passage of time *as* history. In an ironic sense, therefore, David Bosch rightly asserts that "Jewish apocalyptic spells the end of the earlier dynamic understanding of history" (Bosch 1991:20).[27] Jewish apocalyptic most definitely did spell (out) the end(s) of Israel's earlier dynamic understanding of history. Its vivid metaphoric imagery continued to plot the course that the covenant community was to steer as it made its way through history toward the city that is to come.

To be sure, apocalyptic writings regularly divided history into the exile of the present age (*ha-'olam hazeh*), when the wicked flourish and Israel languishes under the rule of idolatrous powers, and the age to come (*ha-'olam haba'*), the time of Israel's vindication as a consequence of the restoration of God's sovereignty over all creation. Thus there was the expectation that the present world order would end, for as N. T. Wright notes, "Only such language, as Jeremiah found, could do justice to the terrible events of his day. But the end of the space-time world, no." Extraordinary phenomena — eclipses, earthquakes, and floods — were sometimes seen as portents of momentous sociopolitical events, but this was due to their understanding of the universe "as an interconnected whole." Such events, "including the ones that were expected to come as the climax of YHWH's restoration of Israel, remained within (what we think of as) the this-worldly ambit." Wright correctly concludes that literature, history, and theology "combine to suggest strongly that we must read most apocalyptic literature, both Jewish and Christian, as a complex metaphor-system which invests space-time reality with its full, that is, its theological significance" (Wright 1992b:298f).[28]

There is accordingly no good reason to associate apocalyptic writings with the annihilation of the physical universe. Not only do such "literalist" readings betray a remarkable lack of literary sensibility and sophistication on the part of many modern exegetes (a trait that is shared by both liberals and conservatives); they also serve to create a false sense of distance between ourselves and the social practice of the first Christians that consists of more than simply the passing of the years. The persistence of the supposition that apocalyptically minded Jews and Christians of the first century expected an imminent end to the time-space universe can be attributed in no small measure to the fact that it allows the modern reader to classify much of what is contained in these texts as fundamentally misleading, the conceptual relics of an archaic and superstitious worldview.[29] According to this peculiarly modern viewpoint, if we want to salvage something from the biblical text, we must do so on a hermeneutical basis more in keeping with the governing assumptions of contemporary life.

Another important development within Israel's poetizing memory, and one that appears in close proximity to the rise of apocalypticism in postexilic Judaism, involves the idea of a messianic figure who would bring about the eschatological triumph of God. It would be impossible in the space allotted to trace (much less examine in detail) the emergence and development of this notion through the first century C.E. or to comment extensively on its subsequent interpretation in both Christian and Jewish thought.[30] The initial impetus for the messianic idea was the struggle between the proponents of monarchical unification of the tribes of Israel and those who continued to represent the case for divine kingship. This crisis led eventually to the prophetic designation of the human king of Israel, "the follower of JHWH" (cf. 1 Sam 12:14), as God's "anointed," *meshiach* JHWH (Buber 1967:162). By the time of the first century C.E. the idea could be found in several varieties of Jewish thought, though certainly there was no standard or uniform use of the term. Indeed, as we will now see, the gospel story itself puts the idea into question even while employing it extensively (Wright 1992b:xiv and 1997:481–89).

Jesus: The *Autobasileia*

For the early church, the pivotal images and analogies generated by Israel's poetizing memory of God's kingship converged in the life, death, and resurrection of Jesus of Nazareth. In this one person the knowledge of history as "the dialectic of an asking divinity and an answer-refusing, but nevertheless an answer-attempting humanity, the dialogue whose demand is an *eschaton*" assumed human flesh. All that he said, did, and suffered during his lifetime did not simply presuppose his Jewish heritage. The New Testament consistently presents him, and he seems to have understood himself, as the "living recapitulation of Israel's history. More precisely, Jesus did not merely copy the history of Israel but realized it afresh in terms of his own life and obedience. By so doing, he re-presented not only Israel's past but also its future, what it would come to be through Yahweh's mighty consummating works" (Clapp 1996a:86; cf. Wright 1997:466). Jesus' poetizing re-enactment of Israel's history and mission in his own life, obedience, and work (including what he accomplished in and through his followers), when combined with the promise for Israel's future embodied in his resurrection, signified to his followers nothing less or other than the presence of the kingdom in his person — the *autobasileia.*

This brief synopsis of the relationship between Jesus and the story of his people offers a much-needed restatement of a key component in Anselm's influential account of the atonement (Anselm, *Cur Deus Homo?*). When we interpret the sinless perfection of Jesus' life in terms of the historic life and memory of Israel, what he achieves does not have to do with the satisfaction of medieval honor but with the realization of Israel's mission. Furthermore, what he accomplished was not to remain his alone, because the purpose of the incarnation was principally "to communicate to human beings the idiom, the *logos* of an adequate return [of God's glory to God], so that this could be made universally" (Milbank 1990:398). As a result, we may accurately portray the Christian life as "the life of itinerant Israel over again, with the same trials and temptations ... but the Christian now knows that what was being rehearsed in a preliminary way in the history of Israel was the life of Christ with his faithful followers. Because in Christ the Christians are the new Israel, their life is bound to be a series of variations on the theme of the 'Way' of the Old Israel as it has been summed up for them in Christ" (Tinsley 1960:157).[31]

The differences between Jesus and many of his Jewish contemporaries, and later between the synagogue and the early church, were therefore not the result of Jesus or his followers stripping away the "extraneous" political and social dimensions of the Jewish tradition. Nowhere in the New Testament is Jesus portrayed as setting completely aside the moral and cultic standards of "normative Judaism" (which in any case did not exist in the first century C.E.) and replacing them with an entirely new and depoliticized code of belief and conduct. The Christian movement did, to be sure, relativize and reinterpret the roles that Torah and Temple — the twin pillars of postexilic Judaism — were to play for those "upon whom the ends of the ages have come" (1 Cor. 10:11). Nevertheless, the difference between the early followers of Jesus and their fellow Israelites had to do rather with the very Jewish questions of (1) whether the messianic rule of God had in fact drawn near (Mark 1:15) in the life and ministry of this relatively obscure individual from the Galilean backwaters of Palestine, and (2) what did the nearness of the kingdom mean for his followers, and especially for the many Gentiles who were responding to the announcement of the good news.

According to the accounts given in the New Testament, the new circumstances that arose with the advent of the messianic age introduced several innovative elements into Israel's historic expectations concerning the rule of God. These innovations, however, finally make sense only within

the complex world of first-century Judaism. The new circumstances can be briefly (though far from adequately)
summarized as follows.[32] First, the coming of the kingdom no longer resided in an indefinite future but was now
at hand (in Greek *engiken*), having drawn near in the life
of Jesus of Nazareth. In all he said and did, therefore, he
challenged those whom he met "to abandon their agendas,
including those agendas which appeared to be sanctioned
in, or even demanded by, the Torah and the Prophets. He
summoned them to follow him in a way of being the people
of YHWH which was, according to him, the true though
surprising fulfillment of the whole scriptural story" (Wright
1997:473). The body of Jesus, which refers not simply to his
flesh and bones but to his whole way of being, the messianic
practice of reconciliation and justice, had thus replaced the
Temple as the center of the Jewish world (cf. Mark 14:8,
15:45f; John 2:19ff) (see Belo 1981:211; Myers 1988:406).

Second, the kingdom, which was brought near in and
through Jesus, continued to make its presence known
through the community of his disciples following his resurrection. His body was re-membered in the social practice
of the church. The distinctive character of this community as a *politeia* in its own right entailed a repudiation
of the militaristic nationalism that significant numbers of
Jews in the first century had embraced. The citizens of
the kingdom were to overcome evil, not by taking up the
sword, "but by a *doubly* revolutionary method: turning the
other cheek, going the second mile, the deeply subversive
wisdom of taking up the cross. The agenda which Jesus
mapped out for his followers was the agenda to which he
himself was obedient. This was how the kingdom would
come, how the battle would be won" (Wright 1997:465). In
place of self-defeating nationalism, Jesus' followers ordered

their common life and witness around mutual relations of charity — embodied in practices of forgiveness and reconciliation, and the bearing of one another's burdens — such that the intimate relationships of the *oikos,* the household, became paradigmatic (cf. Mark 10:28–31). In short, the church was to be "a community in which we relate primarily to the neighbour, and every neighbour is mother, brother, sister, spouse" (Milbank 1990:228; cf. Wright 1997:430–32).

The type of fellowship that constituted everyday life within the messianic household was the result of a social practice that developed initially along lines similar to patterns cultivated within the Jewish synagogue, particularly in the dispersion. Baptism marked the beginning of the Christian life, engrafting those who answered Jesus' summons into this new society and its *modus vivendi* with a world still governed by sin and death. Whatever a person was in the world — Jew or Gentile, male or female, slave or free — that identity was relativized (cf. Gal. 3:27f), and he or she received a new identity through one of the gifts of the Spirit (1 Cor. 12:7). Their table fellowship, structured around the Eucharist, extended economic solidarity to all within this new household and also fostered the virtue of hospitality to strangers. Communal patterns of moral accountability combined procedures for nurturing the practice of forgiveness and reconciliation between the members of their fellowship with processes for ethical deliberation and discernment. All told, these corporate activities extended the drawing near of the kingdom in Jesus' earthly ministry to new social contexts, repeating differently (and thus precisely) the story of God's messianic reign. In each case, these human activities were concrete signs that God was at work in the world. Paul therefore admonished the Christians at Philippi to "work out your own salvation with fear and trembling: for it is God who is at work in you, enabling you both to will and to work for his good pleasure" (Phil. 2:12–13) (see Yoder 1992).

As descendants and heirs of God's promise to Abraham and Sarah, these first Christians "looked forward to the city that has foundations, whose architect and builder is God. . . . They confessed that they were strangers and foreigners on the earth, for people who speak this way make clear that they are seeking a homeland . . . they desire a better country, that is, a heavenly one. Therefore God is not ashamed to be called their God; indeed, he has prepared a city for them" (Heb. 11:10, 13–14, 16). The first-century church understood itself to be a definitive sign that the process of gathering together the commonwealth over which the God of Israel would rule at the ends of the ages had already begun in the midst of the present age. The very existence of the Christian community made this destiny known to a fallen world that did not know either what it was — the cherished creation of God — or its ultimate destination — that *polis* which will descend from heaven like a bride adorned for her husband (Rev. 21:2). The early Christians thus referred to themselves as the *ek-klesia*, a people "called out" of the world so that they might be sent back into it as the provisional assembly (*ekklesia*) of this other city.

The ecclesial household fostered relationships that were not restricted to what modern thought labels the "private" sphere. Rather, they were formed in connection with the activities that make up the business of everyday life within any community: building houses, barns, and bridges, tending gardens and sowing crops, selling wares and repairing tools, raising children, and in general contributing to the welfare of the towns and villages where they lived. Early Christians did not assign such matters to the realm of the "secular" while they concentrated on more "spiritual" concerns. Such distinctions were unknown in the ancient world, and most certainly first-century Palestinian Jews would have found them incomprehensible. On the contrary, these activities and relationships not only constituted the "stuff" of their involvement in God's messianic rule over the present age, but also of their participation in the public square of the empire. But their schooling in ecclesial practices provided them with the practical skills and theoretical framework they would need to survive and prosper. These lessons taught them how to live completely in the world and yet at the same time discern the difference between the ersatz goods and virtues of the empire and those fostered around the table of the Lord and witnessed to by the blood of martyrs.

Third, the fact that the kingdom had drawn near in and through the work of Jesus meant that people could now enter it by responding to the proclamation of redemption through repentance and obedient faith. But as the events that followed Jesus' resurrection and ascension clearly indicate, its constituency was no longer made up solely of Jews but included those ransomed "from every tribe and language and people and nation . . . to be a kingdom and priests serving our God, and they will reign on earth" (Rev. 5:9–10). Whereas Jesus himself had primarily concentrated his ministry on "the lost sheep of the house of Israel," the miracles he performed for Gentiles and a Samaritan (cf. Matt. 15:21–28; Mark 8:1–10; Luke 7:1–10) had the practical effect of announcing to those who were "aliens from the commonwealth of Israel, and strangers to the covenants of promise, having no hope and without God in the world" that the time had come when they would no longer be counted as "strangers and aliens, but . . . citizens with the saints and also members of the household of God" (Eph. 2:12, 19).

Finally, the cost that the drawing near of God's reign would exact from those who heeded Jesus' summons to repent and believe (Mark 1:15) was brutally clarified on the cross. Here the confrontation between the age to come and the present age came clearly into focus, not only for Jesus but also for all those who called him Lord. The way of life that both he and his followers practiced in the sight of those who exercised dominion over the world constituted an explicit threat to their authority. Wright notes in this regard that according to "several Jewish retellings of Israel's story, the great themes of exile and restoration, and of the kingdoms of god and the kingdoms of the world, would reach their climax in a great moment of suffering and vindication. The night would get darker and darker, and then the dawn would come. Israel's tribulations would reach their height, and then be exalted. . . . The symbol of suffering was itself a key ingredient within the Jewish expectation of the great deliverance, the great victory" (Wright 1997:465).[33]

When the first Christians reflected on the meaning of Jesus' passion and subsequent triumph over death, "they concluded that the eschatological drama had opened, that the final tribulation had begun with the suffering and death of the Messiah, that the general resurrection had begun with his resurrection" (Allison 1985:170). Jesus' prediction of death and vindication, not simply for himself but also for his followers (Mark 8:31–38, 13:9–13; cf. Matt. 16:21–28, 24:9–14; Luke 9:21–27, 21:12–19), placed his mission and that of his followers firmly within the thematic scope of these narratives. The divine rule had been inaugurated by Jesus' death and resurrection, but the world still awaited its final vindication at the last day. Until then the drama of the two ages would continue, played out in the lives of those "summoned to share in God's sufferings at the hands of a godless world" (Bonhoeffer 1971:361f).

The Way Forward

The significance of the early church's self-understanding and way of life for our day and time is not at all self-evident. In particular, we must be careful not to romanticize primitive Christianity. The church has struggled from the beginning to remain faithful to its identity and mission as the body of Christ. As virtually every book in the New Testament reminds us, the story of the first followers of Jesus is a record of failure as well as faithfulness.[34] This tension is not in spite of the differences between the church and the world, however, but because of it, thus cutting a line through the heart of every Christian. There would be no problem were it not for Christ's summons to be the people of God in the midst of the present age. Nevertheless, there is no golden age of purity to which the church can either appeal or return to avoid the difficult yet indispensable task of taking responsibility for this mission in whatever settings God chooses to place it. There is no way back; there is only the way forward.

Having said this, it is nonetheless the case that the mission of the church became much more difficult to perform as a result of certain changes that occurred over time. These changes shackled the church's ability to name and remember history as the dialectic of an asking God (whose claim upon Israel, and through them upon the world, finally takes human form in Jesus of Nazareth) and an answer-attempting humanity (whose response to the divine claim takes concrete shape in the church in the power of the Spirit). The practices and conversations within which the identity and mission of this people were initially crafted were deliberately rewoven around a very different set of interlocutors. It is to these social and historical events, grouped together under the rubric of the Constantinian shift, that we now turn our attention.

3

Rendering to Caesar
the Things That Are God's:
The Eclipse of the Church as *Altera Civitas*

The essential nature of the early Christian movement is unintelligible apart from a politics and polity that were, in the words of George Lindbeck, "more Jewish than anything else." The first-century church saw itself as messianic Israel in covenant with the risen Lord, thus continuing the story of Abraham and Sarah's offspring under very distinct circumstances, namely, as those "on whom the ends of the ages have come" (1 Cor. 10:11). Lindbeck also observes that our own time and place in history more closely resembles in many ways the time of Christian beginnings than it does the intervening ages:

> Christendom is passing and Christians are becoming a diaspora. The antagonism of the church to the synagogue has been unmasked (we hope definitively) for the horror it always was. Ecclesial pretensions to fulfillment have become obnoxious to multitudes of Catholics and Protestants alike. Some of the reasons for distorting and then rejecting the scriptural people-

of-God ecclesiology are disappearing, and perhaps its
original version is again applicable.

In short, Lindbeck concludes, there is every reason to return
to Israel's story as the "template" for fashioning an adequate
ecclesiology in and for a "post-Christian" age (Lindbeck
1988:193, 190).

Yet no such return is in sight. For the most part, says
Lindbeck, Christianity remains "as gentile in its self-
understanding as ever, and few Christians are in the least
inclined to think of themselves as even remotely analogous
to a Jewish sect or honorary Jews" (Lindbeck 1988:191).
Particularly foreign to the Jewish tradition is the commonplace notion that "religion" has primarily to do, in Alfred
North Whitehead's famous phrase, with what individuals
do with their solitude, and thus has no direct political rel-
evance. According to Gershom Scholem, "Judaism, in all
of its forms and manifestations, has always maintained a
concept of redemption as an event that takes place publicly,
on the stage of history and within the community." In the
most basic sense of the word, redemption stands "uncon-
ditionally at the end of history as its most distant aim." In
contrast, the sequestering of faith by the later church "as an
event in the spiritual and unseen realm, an event which is
reflected in the soul, in the private world of each individual,
and which effects an inner transformation which need not
correspond to anything outside" (Scholem 1971:1f) more
closely resembles second-century Gnosticism than it does
the messianic politics of Jesus.

Tragically, the Gentile (and thoroughly Gnostic) conception of contemporary Christianity has taken the practice of
the church far from its roots in the people of Israel. John
Yoder goes so far as to suggest that the way of life cul-

tivated by the Jews of the diaspora has been far closer to the messianic ethos of Jesus and his early followers than virtually anything we find in the subsequent history of Christendom (Yoder 1977b and 1985). Although Yoder has probably overstated the case, it would nonetheless be difficult (if not impossible) to deny that significant changes took place somewhere along the line that radically altered the basic premise of the church's self-understanding and *modus vivendi* with the world.

We would do well in this regard to recall what Michael Wyschogrod says about the essential nature of Judaism, that it is "not first a set of ideas but an existing people on whom commands are imposed and from whom ideas are generated but whose own being is the existential soil from which everything else emerges" (Wyschogrod 1983:69). For Jews in the first century the ideas of "monotheism, idolatry, election, holiness, and how these interacted" were not primarily matters for abstract philosophical discussion, but "a shorthand way of articulating the points of pressure, tension and conflict between different actual communities, specifically, Jews and pagans" (Wright 1992a:122).[35] In other words, Judaism is not a worldview that we can compare to alternative intellectual and moral systems in an abstract way, but a particular and altogether comprehensive form of life and community out of which its distinctive convictions arise.

In like fashion, the distinctive social doctrine of early Christianity developed only because there was first a distinguishable Christian social practice "which arose in certain precise historical circumstances, and [which existed] only as a particular historical development" (Milbank 1990:380). This social practice was initially cultivated in the existential soil that is the people of Israel and its narrative memory. With the shift from the polity and politics of early Christianity to the social regime of Christendom, however, the church was increasingly cut off from its formative roots (cf. Rom. 11:17–24).[36] These changes did not take place overnight, nor were they the invidious results of a well-planned conspiracy. In some respects they represented, at least at the outset, a continuation of the distinctive ecclesial practice of apostolic Christianity. Nevertheless, what occurred eventually resulted in the substitution of another social or political "template" for that which had nourished the Jewish people (including the first Christians) for centuries. In what follows, therefore, we will examine the historical developments, often grouped together under the rubric of the Constantinian shift,[37] that brought about this profound shift in the social practice and doctrine of Christianity.

The Church After Constantine

Christians constituted a distinct minority in the empire prior to the reign of Constantine. Recent estimates place the percentage of Christians in the empire around 300 C.E. at about 10 percent (Stark 1996:7). Like Jews in the diaspora, their "distinctive religious scruples made the issue of assimilation and identity, which every immigrant group faced, peculiarly uncomfortable and potentially dangerous" (Meeks 1993:13). It took a certain amount of conviction to align oneself with a group of people that was widely regarded by the Romans as a mischievous and seditious superstition. Conversion was not a private matter between the individual and God, but a social act with profound political repercussions. Add the intermittent threat of persecution to the more mundane problems that invariably come with minority immigrant status, and we can conclude that "cheap grace" was not a widespread problem among the faithful (Yoder 1984:136). In the years that followed the change of heart on the part of emperor and empire, however, the composition and character of the church changed quickly and dramatically. At the first signs of imperial favor, followed a few decades later by recognition as the official religion of Rome, increasing numbers of people presented themselves to the church for baptism. Within a relatively short span of time being a Christian was the accepted norm of imperial society (by the middle of the fourth century C.E. over 50 percent of the population had been baptized) (Stark 1996:7).

Ironically, the initial impetus for the idea of Christendom was the very eschatology that originally put the church and Rome at odds with each other. The wellspring of the early antagonism between the church and the *pax romana* was not (as some have alleged) a world-denying faith on the part of Christianity, inspired by apocalyptic visions of the imminent end of the physical universe. The source of the enmity lay instead, says Alexander Schmemann, in "a highly 'positive' experience of the Kingdom" that entailed a particular way of assessing the world and its constitutive tendencies. The church's "ultimate content and term of reference was not the world but the Kingdom of God, and thus rather than being 'anti-world' it was . . . 'pro-Kingdom.'" The eschatological reign of Israel's God, "announced, inaugurated and given by and in Christ," permeated the early church's mode of practice and governed its antinomical relationship with the world (Schmemann 1979:28f; see also Guroian 1987:119–24).

This antinomy between church and world therefore did not rest upon any kind of ontological dichotomy, for the early Christians confessed that the risen Christ was (all appearances to the contrary notwithstanding) Lord over all creation. They thus could and did speak an emphatic no and an equally emphatic yes to the world. On the one hand, the drawing near of the kingdom of God revealed that the violence and injustice of this world had reached its end (that is, its limit in the divine reign). Because the world rejected the rule of God by condemning Christ to death, "it has condemned itself to die, to be the world whose form and image 'fade away' so that the Kingdom of God 'is not of this world.' This is the Christian no to the world and, from the first day, Christianity proclaimed the end of 'this world' and required from those who believe in Christ and want to partake of his Kingdom that they be 'dead with Christ' and their true life be 'hid with Christ in God.'" On the other hand, the church also proclaimed that the world, creation in rebellion, is redeemed and recreated in Christ, and thus finds its true end (that is, its goal and purpose) in him and his ecclesial body: "This means that for those who believe in Christ and are united to Him, this very world — its time and matter, its life, and even death — have become the 'means' of communion with the Kingdom of God, the sacrament, i.e., the mode, of its coming and presence among men" (Schmemann 1979:29f).

The church and the world are from this standpoint intimately related, but we will misconstrue this relationship if we attempt to distinguish them under the standard categories of sacred and secular. Nor will it do simply to label the former an eschatological community and the other a sociological entity, which serves only to vacate the historical Christian community of any real significance.[38] Both church and world are rather secular realities, in the original sense of that term. The Latin *saeculum* did not designate a space or realm separate from the religious or sacred, but a time. Early Christian writers used the term to refer to the temporal period between fall and eschaton, and after the coming of Christ to the overlap of the two ages in the here and now. The secular thus denotes that period in the story of creation "where coercive justice, private property and impaired natural reason . . . cope with the unredeemed effects of sinful humanity" (Milbank 1990:9).[39] The term that is properly juxtaposed to the idea of the secular in this context "is not 'sacred,' nor 'spiritual,' but 'eternal'" (O'Donovan 1996:211). The "world" designates the social configuration of the present age, creation consigned to futility in hope (Rom. 8:20). The church as parallel *polis,* as a city-within-a city, is the social configuration that concretely signifies to the world its destiny in the age to come. In the words of Augustine, the church is the world reconciled: *mundus reconciliatus Ecclesia* (Augustine as cited in Markus 1970:105).

Ecclesial practice, which continued the dramatic narrative of Israel under new circumstances, thus generated the theoretical standpoint from which Christians interpreted history as a dialectic between God (whose claim upon the world takes human form in the crucified and risen Christ) and rebellious humanity. From this vantage point the role that civil authorities such as Caesar played in history was relativized in keeping with the Old Testament and rabbinic tradition. Rome was not the determinative player on the stage of creation that it claimed to be, but a supporting member of the cast. Together with the other *exousiai* (powers) that govern the present age, it served a limited but specific function. It was to help preserve a rebellious and chaotic world "by encouraging the good and restraining evil, i.e., to serve peace, to preserve the social cohesion in which the leaven of the gospel can build the church, and

also render the old aeon more tolerable" (Yoder 1977a:72f).
Like the Torah of Israel, the church regarded the empire
as a "disciplinarian until Christ came, so that we might be
justified by faith" (Gal. 3:24).

The church thus interpreted the empire typologically,
together with all other powers and rulers that belong to
this age, as both anticipations and refusals of the city of
God (see Milbank 1990:6, 246, 331). As a consequence,
the explicit paganism of Roman statecraft, art, economics, and learning did not negate their ultimate subordination
to Christ. The church's profession of Christ's lordship over
these rulers and powers authorized it "in and in spite of its
distinctness from the world, to speak to the world in God's
name, not only in evangelism but in ethical judgment as
well. The church could take on a prophetic responsibility
for civil ethics without baptizing the state or the statesman. The justice the church demanded of the state was
not Christian righteousness but human *iustitia;* this it could
demand from pagans, not because of any belief in a universal, innate moral sense, but because of its faith in the
Lord." Certain tasks were thus relegated to civil authorities
and structures, because they were also under the sovereignty
of God's messianic reign (Yoder 1994b:56).

With the conversion of Constantine, however, the
church faced a new situation for which it was largely unpre-
pared. The same empire that had regularly ridiculed (and
from time to time persecuted) the members of Christ's
body was now expressing interest in their story of salvation
and its criteria of true universality, even to the point of
inviting the church to order the imperial household. Oliver
O'Donovan, in a sterling apology for the idea of Christendom, rightly notes that this idea was at the outset a
response to the Gentile mission of the church, "constituted

not by the church's seizing alien power, but by alien power's becoming attentive to the church." In other words, the Christendom idea initially presupposed the eschatology of the early church, with its missional vis-à-vis of church and secular rule as distinct structures belonging to two distinct societies or cities: "Until the end of the patristic period this vis-à-vis is constantly in evidence, and the meaning of the Christian empire as a *capitulation* to the throne of Christ is not forgotten" (O'Donovan 1996:195f).

Not surprisingly, the church responded to its new situation "by accepting this invitation to render a 'holy service' for the world" (Guroian 1987:122). Christian jubilation over the Constantinian and Theodosian establishment of a Christian empire was, as O'Donovan and R. A. Markus point out, a continuation of the church's missional confidence in the triumph of God over the rulers and idols of this age (O'Donovan 1996:193ff; Markus 1970:31).[40] The church thus set out to exorcise the world of its demonic powers, to liberate the empire from the thralldom of the "prince of the air"; in short, to make "this world 'new' before God by the power of the Holy Spirit." The church of early Christendom sought to serve the world while remaining true to its identity as the sacrament of the kingdom, "God's eschatological vehicle of passage for this world through time into the world to come." Unfortunately it failed in the attempt, and in spite of its best intentions the blame rests largely with the church, because in the end it "endeavored to be not what it is but what it is not" (Guroian 1987:122).

In its eagerness to perform this holy service for the world, Christians fell prey to a radically realized eschatology, thus effacing most of the meaningful distinctions that it had formerly cultivated between itself and the world as distinct political societies. The church, in an ironic and tragic inversion of the teaching of Jesus, began (unwittingly at first, overwhelmed by the incredible changes that had taken place in the empire) to render to Caesar what belonged to God.[41] Eusebius of Caesarea, who wrote several orations in praise of Constantine, went so far as to say that God had rewarded Constantine "with such long-lasting honors that not even three ten-year periods suffice for his rule, but instead He bestows it for as long as possible, and extends it even into far distant eternity."[42] He also re-narrated several Old Testament passages, traditionally interpreted as messianic prophecies, as allusions to the emperor:

> For at one and the same time that the error of the demons was refuted, the eternal enmity and warfare of the nations was resolved. Moreover, as One God and one knowledge of this God was heralded to all, one empire waxed strong among men, and the entire race of mankind was redirected into peace and friendship as all acknowledged each other brothers and discovered their related nature. . . . Thus the predictions of the ancient oracles and utterances of the prophets were fulfilled — countless of them not time now to quote, but including those which said of the saving Logos that "He shall have dominion from sea to sea, and from the rivers unto the ends of the earth." And again, "In his days shall the righteous flourish and abundance of peace." "And they shall beat their swords into ploughshares, and their spears into pruning hooks: nation shall not lift up sword against nation, neither shall they learn war any more" (Eusebius, *In Praise of Constantine* 16, 7–8).[43]

Eusebius structurally identified the Constantinian moment with the victory of God, even the Parousia, with Constantine as a kind of Christ-surrogate: "The divine rule, with all its attributes, had become luminously present in the royal man. It is as though the eschatological horizon of all political theology has, in the moment of astonishment, come to be spoken of as present" (O'Donovan 1996:198).

Eusebius was not alone in asserting that Roman supremacy had united the whole world under the rule of Christ. According to Prudentius, who wrote in the latter half of the fourth century, a new era had begun with the submission of the empire to Christ, establishing a time that shall know no end: "The world receives you now, O Christ, the world which is held in the bonds of harmony by peace and by Rome. These you have appointed to be the chief and highest powers in the world. Nor does Rome please thee without peace; and it is only Roman excellence that ensures a lasting peace" (Prudentius as cited by Markus 1970:28). As these statements indicate, the image of the millennium in the Apocalypse of John was sundered from the future and applied to the present, as secular rule was increasingly looked upon "as if the Kingdom of God had already appeared 'in power' and as if the empire were the manifestation of this power in the world and in history" (Meyendorff 1979:214). When this near-identification of world and church is made, all God could possibly have in store for the future is more of what has already been achieved (Yoder 1984:137). The Jewish polity and politics of the kingdom were already well down the road to becoming the Gentile servant of imperial policy.

There were those, to be sure, who sought over the centuries to recover the future horizon and the boundary between God and the emperor, while at the same time seeking to come to terms with the dramatic changes that had taken place. Augustine, for example, had been prepared for a decade or more to embrace the concept of an *imperium Christianum* as a decisive fulfillment of God's promises foretold in the Old Testament prophecies: "The few pagans that remain fail to realise the wonder of what is happening. ...Now the God of Israel himself is destroying the idols of the heathen.... Through Christ the king he has subjugated the Roman empire to the worship of his name; and he has converted it to the defence and service of the Christian faith, so that the idols, on account of whose cult his sacred mysteries had previously been rejected, should now be destroyed" (Augustine as cited in Markus 1970:30). Augustine thus for a time inscribed the empire, and of more importance the Christian emperor, onto the pages of sacred history.

But around the year 400 we can discern a radical transformation in Augustine's thinking, as he began to repudiate the ideas that he had formerly put forward to justify the idea of a Christian empire (a notion that had conflicted at any rate with his homogenous view of history from Incarnation to Parousia) and the use of coercion in the legal repression of paganism and heresy. Augustine came to the realization that the church, the pilgrim city of God, could never enter into a concordat with the earthly city, whether Theodosius' Rome or any other political entity of the *saeculum.* According to Markus, O'Donovan's advocacy of a "Christian secular political order" (1996:195) would have struck the mature Augustine as "a category mistake. ...The Gospel can never be at home in the world, and cannot fail to bring a true believer into conflict with any existing order of things. It is in essential and permanent tension with the world" (Markus 1970:126, 169; see also

Williams 1987). Augustine came to believe that the politics and polity of the church represented an insubordinate challenge to secular rulers of the world.

Guided by his mentor in these matters, the Donatist theologian Tyconius, Augustine concluded in *City of God* that whereas the heavenly city is on pilgrimage in this world, calling out citizens from all nations and so collecting a society of aliens speaking all languages, she "takes no account of any difference in customs, laws, and institutions, by which earthly peace is achieved and preserved — not that she annuls or abolishes any of those, rather, she maintains them and follows them ... provided that no hindrance is presented thereby to the religion which teaches that the one supreme and true God is to be worshipped" (Augustine, *City of God* 19.17).[44] As a result of this shift in his thinking, by the end of his life Augustine, "almost alone among his contemporaries," managed to break the spell of a Christianized empire or secular social order. He labored diligently in his later writings to keep alive "a cast of mind, a theology, a conception of the Church and of its place in the world, which [it] had discarded in 313" (Markus 1970:42, 132).[45]

Nevertheless, ecclesiastical leaders in the West as a rule did not follow Augustine's lead (though they thought that was precisely what they were doing). Instead, they took advantage of the collapse of imperial structures in the fifth and sixth centuries to negotiate with the Germanic kingdoms that replaced the empire for separate juridical status, complete with their own authority and jurisdiction in this world. Pope Gelasius moved Christendom further down the road to a unified body politic, with the church as its "soul," when he assimilated the traditional demarcation between the two ages to the distinction between priest and king, who would jointly rule the world, each according to his proper office. The duality of kingdoms that in the early church had distinguished the present age from the age to come became a duality of government. Sacred and secular officials were now to rule cooperatively within one universal society. Society traveled still further down this path during the Carolingian age when the emphasis in this allocation of roles between priest and king was changed from their joint rule of the world to that of the church. O'Donovan notes that "with the change from 'world' to 'church'... the last consciousness of a notional distinction between the two societies had disappeared; one could no longer say that the ruler ruled Christians *qua* civil society but not *qua* heavenly city." The king "now exercised his office of ruling wholly within the church, as a kind of lay ministry or charism. Later, his governing role came to seem an essential safeguard for lay ministry against clerical domination" (O'Donovan 1996:204, 212).

And so bishop and pope began to collaborate actively with civil authorities to administer the constantly evolving social order of Christendom. This joint administration reached its culmination during the Middle Ages when the church was officially recognized as the supreme authority, while civil rulers became in effect, as John Figgis puts it, "the police department of the Church" (Figgis 1956:4). In this schema the church effectively had no independent *raison d'être*, but existed as the active principle of the world, enabling the earthly city to achieve its own *telos*, as measured by its own standards. The content of this joint administration, not surprisingly, was largely derived from pagan modes of practice, as seen in Anselm's telling re-narration of the atoning work of Christ in *Cur Deus Homo?*[46] This venture into civil government reached its apex in the eleventh century during the papacy of Gregory VII, when the church hierarchy extracted from the right of property as set forth in Roman and feudal law the theory of "the absolute and universal jurisdiction of the supreme authority, and developed it into the doctrine of the *plenitudo potestatis* of the Pope" (Figgis 1956:4; cf. O'Donovan 1996:206).

Christendom developed in a somewhat different manner in the East. The Orthodox Church did not have a juridical agreement with the empire that defined for both parties their respective rights and responsibilities. A christological pattern prevailed instead, according to which there was the union of divine and the human in the single entity of the Christian empire, which was seen as "the image of the person of Christ who is the 'unique source of the . . . civil and ecclesiastical hierarchies.'" The "symphony" that was to take place between "divine things" and "human affairs" did not result in a joint administration of society by two institutionally distinct subjects of power as it did in the West. There was instead, as Schmemann puts it, "an interpenetration of the Church and the empire, of their structures and functions . . . comparable to that of the soul and the body" (Schmemann 1979:69).[47] The Caesaropapism that distinguished the Byzantine "symphony" from its Western counterpart thus had only one subject, the Christian empire, and church authorities for all intents and purposes occupied a department within that empire.

It is important to note that although the institutional arrangements that emerged in the West did entangle the church's eschatological mission within the idolatrous presumptions of imperial power, they did have their advantages when compared with subsequent developments in the post-Reformation era. Milbank points out that the "externality of the imperial *potestas* with regard to the Church (whereby only the ruler, not the empire as such, was wholly *within* the

Church) was maintained to register the imperfectly Christian character of the empire, and the realm of *res divinae* over which the Church was sovereign was certainly not confined to matters of 'private' salvation as the modern age might conceive them" (Milbank 1990:96). As a consequence of its distinctive juridical status, the church hierarchy possessed a certain independence in its relationship with the civil authorities.

John Yoder — a Mennonite who can scarcely be accused of nostalgia for the good old days of Christendom — concurs with Milbank on this point: "The [ecclesiastical] hierarchy had a power base and a self-definition which enabled independent judgment. An emperor or a prince could really be forced to listen to the bishop by the ban or interdict. The criteria of just war theory and other limits on the prerogatives of princes (the rules of chivalry, the Peace of God, the civil exemptions of the clergy, the immunities of pilgrims) had real effect" (Yoder 1984:144). For all the flaws, the medieval arrangement between civil and ecclesiastical authorities did grant to the church the institutional freedom and wherewithal to bring influence to bear on those who wielded power.

The juridical arrangement between the church and civil authorities in the West remained largely in place until shortly before the time of the Reformation, when social changes began to undercut the ability of ecclesiastical authorities to limit secular power effectively. The dominance exercised by the church hierarchy over the civil rulers in medieval society was sharply inverted during the sixteenth and seventeenth centuries. The means for making this inversion came in the creation of the modern state, "a form of public power separate from both ruler and the ruled, and constituting the supreme political authority within a certain defined territory" (Skinner 1978:353).[48] In both Roman Catholic and Protestant countries the church was relieved of its separate jurisdictional authority and redefined as a purely suasive body, allowing the state to become the absolute and unquestioned political authority within the (often arbitrary) boundaries that defined its territory. When the church lost the independent political and moral authority to demand that civil rulers account for their actions, its ability to affect its social context quickly began to erode as well. Unfortunately, those who maneuvered to rule these new political entities proved to be far more adept than ecclesiastical leaders at manipulating doctrinal disputes and confessional loyalties in their ascent to power.[49]

The Rise of Christendom and the Eclipse of the Christian Mission

It would be hard to overestimate the long-term effects that the Constantinian shift had on both church and empire. Insofar as the latter is concerned, Charles Cochrane notes ironically that if Constantine was deliberately weaving a spider's web for Christianity, his plan failed miserably, because "it was destined, by destroying his successors, to ruin his own dynastic hopes" (Cochrane 1940:211). Perhaps the pagan critics of the church in the fourth century, who accused Christianity of undermining the foundations of the empire, were right after all. It may well be that empires cannot be sustained for very long without propitiating the spirits of this age. If you believe that the *modus operandi* of empires is necessary for the welfare of humankind, then the Constantinian shift was in fact a fatal error in judgment.

At stake for the church, by contrast, was its carefully nurtured distinction between itself and world, and thus between the present age and the age to come. On this distinction its identity and mission were predicated from the beginning. Before Constantine everyone, believer and nonbeliever alike, knew that the church existed, but they had to believe against appearances that the risen Christ ruled the cosmos (Yoder 1994b:57). The mode of life cultivated by this community before the world constituted the principal sign of Christ's lordship to the world: "Through the church the wisdom of God in its rich variety [is] made known to the rulers and authorities in the heavenly places" (Eph. 3:10). From the standpoint of the New Testament, then, the body of Christ, not the rulers and powers of the present age, was the primary bearer of the meaning of history. But with the conversion of Constantine, differentiation between the two cities was gradually sacrificed to the demands of the one society of Christendom, with the church cast in the role of its spiritual form. As a result, the mission of the church, "to be at the disposal of the Holy Spirit in making Christ's victory known" (O'Donovan 1996:214),[50] was increasingly placed in jeopardy.

The missional character of the church thus undergoes a decided change after the conversion of Constantine. Because the emperor and (to some degree) the empire were now Christian, the rule of Christ was now readily manifest to all in the person and power of Caesar. As a consequence, the carefully drawn distinctions between the world and the church, the present age and the age to come, were largely (though not completely) fused into one entity, the *corpus christianum*. The eventual result of this near-fusion was the loss of focus on the church's missionary identity. This loss is ironic as well as tragic, because the idea of Christendom originated in the church's understanding of mission. As O'Donovan puts it, it was "the missionary imperative that compelled the church to take the conversion of the empire seriously and to seize the opportunities it offered. These were not merely opportunities for 'power.' They were opportunities for preaching the Gospel, baptising believers, curbing the violence and cruelty of empire and, perhaps most important of all, forgiving their former persecutors." But as the two cities merged into one grand society, it became increasingly difficult to see the partnership between ecclesiastical and civil authorities in terms of God's messianic kingdom. One could be forgiven, says O'Donovan, if it seemed as though "there was no more mission to be done. The peril of the Christendom idea . . . was that of negative collusion: the pretence that there was no further challenge to be issued to the rulers in the name of the ruling Christ" (O'Donovan 1996:212f).

Whatever it was originally designed to be, the long-term effect of the Constantinian shift was to radically redefine the church's identity and vocation. The idea of mission no longer denoted what the church was originally called to be, an outpost of heaven living as aliens in a strange land, calling the powers and principalities to account in the name of the risen Lord who ruled over all creation, and gathering together in the power of the Spirit the first members of a new humanity, who through repentance and faith were being recreated according to the image of God's servant-messiah. Although on one level it could appear as though there was no more mission to be done within the Christian empire, on another level the notion of mission meant consolidating the respective jurisdictions of ecclesiastical and civil institutions within the new society. Ambrose, a fourth-century bishop of Milan, successfully exerted ecclesial authority over Theodosius I on more than one occasion. Even more telling is the fact that the legal mechanisms of the empire that once had persecuted Christians now swung into action to suppress paganism and enforce doctrinal orthodoxy. What had once been achieved solely on the basis of the truthful testimony of believers and the blood of the martyrs was now the responsibility of those who wielded the coercive powers of the earthly city. And whereas it once took courage to cast one's lot with a persecuted sect, after 313 C.E. "it would take exceptional conviction not to be counted as a Christian" (Yoder 1984:136).

The internal consolidation of the *corpus christianum* further blurred the distinction between the two powers or "swords." In the ninth century Charlemagne took full advantage of the confidence shown to him by the church to invest his rule with sacral authority. He effectively saw himself, "without incongruity, as a kind of bishop with a sword, and his court theologians no longer talk, like Pope Gelasius, of two powers, imperial *potestas* and ecclesial *auctoritas* within one *mundus,* but of *potestas* and *auctoritas* within the single *ecclesia*" (Milbank 1990:419; cf. O'Donovan 1996:203–205). This mixing of piety and power was not limited to the Carolingian empire. In virtually every part of the world Christendom reached — not only in the "Old World," but also in the "New World" of Africa, Asia, and the Americas — it bound saving faith tightly together with loyalty to nation and ruler. In the words of the sixteenth-century Dominican Bartolomé de Las Casas, the colonial powers "baptized their execrable tyrannies, ambitions, and acts of greed" (de Las Casas as cited in Gutiérrez 1993:106).

Beyond the limits of the territory controlled by Rome, mission became synonymous with imperial expansion. Cochrane notes that from Constantine's standpoint, the preservation of ecclesiastical unity at Nicaea in 325 C.E.

"contained the promise of even more spectacular achievement, in the shape of an empire bigger and better than
that of Augustus Caesar himself. For in the evangeliza-
tion of Germans and Orientals, the emperor discerned the
beginning of a new and significant phase of international
relationships" (Cochrane 1940:210f). Many of the peoples
of the East remained beyond Christendom's grasp, particularly after the rise of Islam, but the Germanic tribes to the
North were successfully "evangelized" and eventually incorporated into a "Holy" Roman Empire, a name that first
circulated in the court of Emperor Frederick Barbarossa
(1152–90).

As this process of internal consolidation and external
expansion continued, the outsider, the other, the non-
Christian ceased to be the single most significant measure
of that charity or love that is formed through participation in the justice of God's reign (cf. Matt. 5:43–48; Luke
6:32–36). He or she became either the barbarian who could
therefore be largely ignored or the heretic who must be pun-
ished. By the time we get to the era of the Crusades, he or
she was the "infidel," the person in whom all that is opposed
to the virtues of faith, hope, and love was to be found. Mission had now become holy war. To destroy the infidels, "or
to give one's life in the attempt, [became] a positively vir-
tuous undertaking, quite without regard for the ordinary
criteria of justifiable violence (the so-called just war theory).
Our world has a divinely imparted duty to destroy or rule
over their world" (Yoder 1984:138).

The Constantinian effacement of the political distinction between world and church, between the present age
and the age to come, did not cease with the fall of Rome
in the West or with the collapse of the medieval synthesis, but continues unabated through Christian history down

to the present day. The magisterial Reformers, for all of their revolutionary insight into the fallen nature of the medieval church, did not question the division of labor between ecclesiastical and civic authorities that had marked the Middle Ages. They did, however, add one innovative element to their otherwise conservative policy. They aligned their movements with the rulers of a new type of political entity that proclaimed its sovereignty absolute — the nation-state. This move not only undermined the transnational and ecumenical character of the Roman Catholic Church; it also effectively (though unwittingly) provided the ideological props for modern politics. The immediate effect of this alignment of Christian piety and national allegiance was to fan the flames of national and ethnic hatred that burned out of control in what are erroneously called the Wars of Religion.[51]

Within Protestantism the so-called free churches, represented most ably by Baptists in North America, thought they had finally liberated Christian faith from all political entanglements by agreeing to the institutional separation of church and state proposed by the leading figures of the Enlightenment. However, what often goes unnoticed is that the formal separation of these institutions took place under the auspices of a social arrangement that sanctioned a moral and cultural identity between mainline Protestant Christianity and the liberal nation-state. Alexis de Tocqueville called attention to this unique synthesis of Protestantism and Enlightenment liberalism in American civil society:

> While the law allows the American people to do what they please, religion prevents them from conceiving, and forbids them to commit what is rash and unjust.

Religion in America takes no direct part in the government of society, but it must be regarded as the first of their political institutions; for if it does not impart a taste for freedom, it facilitates the use of it. I do not know whether all Americans have a sincere faith in their religion...but I am certain that they hold it to be indispensable to the maintenance of republican institutions (de Tocqueville 1945:316; as cited by Guroian 1994:88).

In such a context, church and state are indeed separated at the institutional level, but their respective spheres of influence are reintegrated within a social order driven finally by political and economic forces that recognize no ethical or religious limits to their authority. And so, although the state claims a de jure neutrality concerning religion, it nonetheless presides "over a de facto integration of Protestant piety, belief, and polity within the democratic ethos" (Guroian 1994:88). The mission of the church within this arrangement is to help the state and other social institutions maintain a harmonious social equilibrium.[52]

Not surprisingly, the ethical conduct expected of Christians also changed substantially after Constantine. O'Donovan's protests notwithstanding, the conversion of pagan rulers did not leave the missional vis-à-vis between the church and the world "exactly where it was" (O'Donovan 1996:196). As we have seen, Christian history was renarrated in the decades following the conversion of Constantine, with a few crucial exceptions, as the story of the convergence of monotheism and monarchy in the person of the emperor. The Christian ruler and his ministers (not the ascetic, the martyr, or even the ordinary believer struggling in the course of everyday life to remain faithful to the

risen Lord) became the paradigm for moral discernment.
The question that concerned theologians and clergy was no
longer "How can we survive and remain faithful Christians
under Caesar?" but instead became "How can we adjust the
church's expectations so that Caesar can consider himself
a faithful Christian?" (Clapp 1996:26)[53] The practices and
disciplines that had once distinguished the church as a distinctive *politeia* figured less and less in the determination
of moral standards. Criteria more suited to the church's
newly acquired standing in the world would substantially
reconfigure the sense and sensibility of these practices.

The demise of monarchy over the last few centuries as
the preferred form of government in the West has not resulted in the rollback of Constantinianism as such, nor has
it reestablished first-century moral norms in the church.
The reinscription of the Christian narrative onto the pages
of history continues unabated, not as the story of the convergence of monotheism and monarchy, but rather as the
confluence of monotheism and democratic nationalism, or
monotheism and capitalist markets. "Radical monotheism"
and "Western culture" have now become virtually synonymous in the minds of both professional theologians and
people in the pew.[54] Perhaps the most explicit statement
of this latter-day convergence is to be found in a seminal work by an early twentieth-century theologian, E. Y.
Mullins. Mullins boldly compares what he considers to be
the "axioms" of all true religion with

> a stalactite descending from heaven to earth, formed
> by the deposits from the water of life flowing out
> of the throne of God down to mankind, while our
> American political society is the stalagmite with its
> base upon the earth rising to meet the stalactite and

formed by deposits from the same life-giving stream. When the two shall meet, then heaven and earth will be joined together and the kingdom of God will have come among men. This is the process that runs through the ages (Mullins 1908:274).[55]

In such circumstances the practices and habits of discipleship as established by the words and actions of Jesus and the disciplines of the early church no longer play the leading role in determining the ethical requirements of the Christian life, at least for most people. Moral guidelines are restructured to accommodate the duties and obligations of station, office, and profession, that is, social roles established and maintained by the ruling authorities of the world so that they could serve their preservative function. With the church's change of status under Constantine, these responsibilities were now to be exercised predominantly (and within a few centuries exclusively) by Christians. "In a real sense," says Rodney Clapp, "it becomes fine and commendable for professing Christians to participate in the state and other realms of culture as if the lordship of Christ made no concrete difference. Even for Christians, culture begins to be seen as autonomous, as holding its own key to its establishment, maintenance and true purposes" (Clapp 1996a:26).

The reworking of moral rectitude around these worldly vocations required a considerable degree of adjustment, because the early church regarded many of them as antithetical to the demands of the messianic reign inaugurated by Jesus. Nevertheless, since the time of Constantine most people have not been held to the standards of the New Testament, because empire and feudal kingdom (and later nation-state and commercial market) required their skills and talents to function. Pagan standards related to the ownership and right of property, the duties of the soldier, the civil and market expertise provided by the guilds, the craft of the statesman, and even marriage were incorporated into the church's moral practice and instruction. The comprehensive way of life once signified by baptism and the other practices and disciplines of the community was increasingly reserved for the vocation of the "religious," that is, members of monastic orders.

The decisive shift in the church's mission and ethical standards has been accompanied by a radical redefinition of the ideas of faith and grace. In the apostolic church these notions were unintelligible apart from the community's diplomatic mission, which was to represent the rule of the God of Israel to the authorities and rulers of this age. This mission was not merely conceptual, but was embodied in a communal form of life sustained by the practices of baptism, eucharistic solidarity, communal discernment, and mutual admonition and correction. As such, faith and grace were, in Bonhoeffer's words, "always concerned with *anthropos teleios,* the whole man, even where, as in the Sermon on the Mount, the decalogue is pressed home to refer to 'inward disposition.' That a good 'disposition' can take the place of total goodness is quite unbiblical" (Bonhoeffer 1971:346). In the thinking of early Christianity, moreover, the "whole person" to which the Bible refers did not exist apart from the community of faith and its peculiar network of social relationships, and thus not apart from its understanding of (and involvement in) the kingdom of God.

As its identity as a people on pilgrimage to another city began to fade in the years following Constantine, the church underwent a transformation that (especially in the

West) would reconstitute it as an institution that attends solely to what goes on within the soul. The conduct of the body in the public square was thus left to the charge of civil authorities. The ramifications of this transformation were immense. As Bonhoeffer observes, the "displacement of God from the world, and from the public part of human life, led to the attempt to keep his place secure at least in the sphere of the 'personal,' the 'inner', and the 'private'" (Bonhoeffer 1971:344). Christian self-identity has thus been effectively divorced from the practices and virtues that give sense and direction to one's interaction with the world, and gradually reconfigured as something that was essentially inward and private, something that begins and ends in the interior life of each individual. This trend is especially evident in Puritanism, where "the idea that emotional states had a special spiritual significance and that consequently certain displays of feeling were to be considered as signs of godliness was to outlast the collapse of Calvinism as a coherent theological system" (Campbell 1987:127).[56]

As noted above, in the Middle Ages so-called public expressions of faith were increasingly reserved for those who took clerical vows and monastic orders. Although these orders helped preserve something of the distinctive pattern of life that once set the church apart in the eyes of the Romans,[57] they also helped to foster a dubious moral dualism, with the "evangelical counsels" for themselves and the less demanding "precepts" for everybody else. This dual standard not only fostered the illusion that monastics formed an ascetic elite that achieved perfection through self-denial; it also made the connection of secular Christian existence with a way of life that was once expected of everyone in the church more and more tenuous.[58] As the centuries went by, most Christians increasingly lost sight of the relationship between the grace that is freely given (*gratia gratis data*) and the grace that makes pleasing (*gratia gratis faciens*). Bonhoeffer aptly names this separation the doctrine of cheap grace, which is "grace sold on the market like cheapjack's wares." In this doctrine, says Bonhoeffer, "the world finds a cheap covering for its sins; no contrition is required, still less any real desire to be delivered from sin. Cheap grace therefore amounts to a denial of the living Word of God, in fact, a denial of the Incarnation of the Word of God. Cheap grace means the justification of sin without the justification of the sinner" (Bonhoeffer 1959:45f).

The magisterial Reformers and their ecclesiastical offspring tried to counter the effects of this dualism by rejecting the medieval conception of monasticism as a higher form of life and lifting up "ordinary life" as the proper venue for glorifying God. But when they did so they inadvertently increased the gap between the early church's understanding of life under the messianic rule of Christ and what is deemed normative for present-day believers. The resulting conception of ordinary life, originally formulated by the Puritans, further reinforced the interiorization and individualization of faith as well as the accommodation of moral standards to the expediencies of worldly occupation. The Puritans advanced the idea that secular vocations in what we now call the modern world have their own intrinsic rules and norms that govern their day-to-day operations. These vocations, in other words, are substantially independent of any sort of ecclesial mediation or adjudication. All that the church may reasonably expect from them is the formal requirement that an individual's employment be deemed "useful to mankind" (but by what standard?) and "imputed to use by God" (but in what ways and to what ends?).[59]

The autonomy of these secular callings also accelerates the privatization of faith within Constantinianism in general, and Protestantism in particular. As we noted above, in the early days of Christendom the question was, "How can we adjust the church's expectations so that Caesar can consider himself a faithful Christian?" With the hallowing of ordinary life the form of the question changes, but its basic tendency remains fixed. We now ask, "How can we adjust the church's expectations so that the politician, entrepreneur, manager, or therapist can consider herself or himself a faithful Christian?" The answer, according to the Puritan conception of vocation, is that the highest life is no longer "defined by an exalted *kind* of activity; it all turns on the *spirit* in which one lives what everyone lives, even the most mundane existence" (Taylor 1989:224; cf. Campbell 1987:99–172). The morality of an individual's actions turns, in short, on her or his intentions alone.

These developments did not take hold simply because they were inherently reasonable as measured by some neutral standard. They did so rather "because they were functional. They explained and justified the growing distance from Jesus and his replacement by other authorities and another political vision than that of the Kingdom of God" (Yoder 1984:141). By the end of the seventeenth century, all that remained of the church's traditional authority was "the purely interior government of the souls of its members; their bodies [were] handed over to the secular authorities" (Cavanaugh 1995:399). As time passed, even that limited jurisdiction was expropriated from the body of Christ. With the privatization of Christian piety, particularly in Protestant communions (a trend reinforced by nineteenth-century Romanticism [Campbell 1987:173–201]), divine forgiveness was effectively transformed into "an individual transaction between God and a particular person, largely devoid of its eschatological context and with virtually no consequences for either Christian community or social and political life" (Jones 1995:38). The church, on this account, was effectively incidental to salvation, an association of believers gathered together for the purpose of propagating the faith.

A Hard Habit to Break

Despite the loss of political independence and moral authority, most Christian communities continue to embrace some form of Constantinianism. The ecclesiastical structures that emerge in the post-Reformation period — both Roman Catholic and Protestant — still by and large hearken back "to the style of the *ancien régime* ... to a society in which the churches regarded themselves as the spiritual form of a material community" (Kent 1982:viii). Most of these groups continue to define themselves and their role in the world according to this social paradigm even as the doctrinal and moral content of latter-day Christendom steadily diminishes to accommodate the expansion of a nominally Christian civil religion "from evangelical consensus to Protestantism-in-general, to Christianity-in-general, to the Judeo-Christian-tradition-in-general, to deism-in-general" (Linder and Pierard 1978:74, as cited in Clapp 1996a:29)[60] and finally now to values-in-general. We thus are confronted with the ironic situation of so many "post-Constantinians" in so-called liberal churches who "proclaim with joy the end of that era, yet ... never hesitate to issue advice to states as if they were Christian kingdoms" (Ramsey 1989:125). Christendom is indeed a hard habit to break (Clapp 1996a:29).

But our analysis of the changes that alter in many and significant ways the *modus vivendi* of the church after Constantine would be incomplete if we stopped here, for with the rise of the modern world a new set of institutions and techniques came onto the scene that transformed but also consolidated and extended the basic tendencies of the Constantinian shift. We must therefore examine certain developments that began in Europe with the Reformation and were institutionalized in both Europe and North America by the Renaissance and the Enlightenment, changes that further distorted the relationship of the ecclesial *altera civitas* to the world. In a very real sense, Constantinianism only forms the backdrop for an even more comprehensive process of social transformation — the Cartesian shift.

4

Romancing Divinity:
The Church and the Risk Culture
of Postmodernity

Historians, philosophers, and theologians routinely refer to
René Descartes as one of the principal architects of the
modern age. One popular introduction to modern philosophy, for example, declares that the French mathematician
and philosopher, insofar as "he deferred to no intellectual
authority other than the 'natural light' of reason" (Scruton
1981:29), was the perfect representative of the new scientific spirit that characterized the age of Enlightenment.
However, we cannot attribute his place in the history books
to any explicit philosophical position or argument he advanced, for later philosophers have shown that virtually all
of them are deficient in some critical way. Nor should we
attribute it to his quest for a method that would provide the
foundation for sure and certain knowledge, though this attempt figured prominently in what he did accomplish. His
well-deserved reputation is due rather to the imaginative
way he spelled out a comprehensive program for a new social order and sensibility, thereby consolidating the hopes of

many in his time and since for "an entirely human order on earth... erected entirely with the help of human capacities and resources alone" (Bauman 1993:23).

Descartes was supremely confident that this program would "make ourselves, as it were, the masters and possessors of nature, which aim is not only to be desired for the invention of an infinity of devices by which we might enjoy, without any effort, the fruits of the earth and all its commodities, but also principally for the preservation of health" (Descartes 1968:78). In the conquest of nature, humankind would eventually make "reason's 'sweet dream' of a heaven on earth" a reality (Poteat 1985:4). However, if human beings were to realize this idyllic vision, Descartes was convinced that we could no longer rely on the moral and intellectual inheritance of countless generations, practices, and institutions attuned by centuries of refinement to the delicate balance between ourselves and the world in which we live. These were too arbitrary and divisive, too unreliable and uncertain to provide the sure and certain foundation required by a world that was to be fashioned solely on the basis of human resources and abilities.

Given the political upheaval and religious turmoil of his day, we can certainly understand why he came to this conclusion. With the bloodshed of the Thirty Years' War that followed the murder of Henry IV of France, "the philosophy of skepticism was a luxury that few people felt able to accept" (Toulmin 1990:69). But the breakdown of authority during the seventeenth century was not simply the result of the so-called wars of religion that were raging all over Europe at the time. Lorraine Daston notes that civility was in equally short supply in the new natural philosophy of the day: "Seventeenth century science was a battlefield where rivals and factions stopped at nothing to scientifically discredit and personally abuse (the two were seldom distinguished) one another" (Daston 1994:52f). That Descartes and his contemporaries yearned for some sense of certainty in a world fraught with considerable unpredictability and great unpleasantness should therefore not come to us as a great surprise.

Descartes decided that anything from the past that was to be carried over and reaffirmed in an enlightened age would have to pass muster at the bar of reason's natural light, to which everyone purportedly had access apart from the uncertain opinions of human traditions. He sincerely believed that by attending to this light the essential human being, or "thinking thing" (res cogitans),[61] could shed all particular commitments and loyalties, and elevate itself onto a very high mountain, as it were, where it could view all the kingdoms of the world in an instant (cf. Matt. 4:8; Luke 4:5). From this lofty perch, "disembrangled from the moil and ruck of the world like discarnate gods" (Poteat 1985:267), humankind could safely and precisely chart the way toward an earthly paradise. And so, like the adolescent lover who does not simply pursue his beloved but passionately desires to possess her, human beings since the time of Descartes have coveted the status of the immortals, and did all that was in their power to charm from the universe the secret of the gods.

At the heart of the Cartesian quest for certainty and its flirtation with divinity is an intense (even obsessive) desire to overcome fate, or at least to drastically limit the role it plays in human affairs. In many respects the defining trait of modernity has been, in the words of Anthony Giddens, "an alteration in the perception of determination and contingency, such that human moral imperatives, natural causes, and chance reign in place of religious cosmologies"

(Giddens 1990:34). This shift in perception, as Giddens puts it, was not simply the result of a new definition of what it means to talk about human beings as rational beings (though this definition played an important role in this little drama), but was equally the product of a vast technical apparatus that now extends to virtually every nook and cranny of both the natural and social worlds. The sole purpose of this technical environment was to liberate humankind as much as possible from the unpredictable and seemingly indifferent hand of fortune.

After three centuries, virtually everybody and every place on the globe have been brought — sometimes willingly, oftentimes not — under the authority of the regime charged with making this vision of a heaven on earth a reality. The movers and shakers of the modern City worked long and hard to divest its body politic of every conviction and practice not directly entailed in its architectonic vision. This process of divestment went rather slowly at first, but it continued to pick up speed as the years went by. We who are the heirs of this particular project are consequently the products not only of criticism and revolution, but also of a self-inflicted amnesia. Seduced by Descartes' depiction of the essential human subject as an ahistorical, disembodied entity for thinking and acting rationally in response to stimuli provided by an "external" environment, the modern world systematically dismantled the "encumbrances" that local customs and conventions "impose" on "autonomous individuals," and in the process deprived us not only of our sense of who we are and what is at stake in our lives, but also what makes for genuine and lasting peace.

Put differently, although the quest to realize the sweet dream of a heaven on earth was certainly responsible for some impressive technical achievements, its "ripening flirtation with godhood" also brought human beings face to face "with infinity, restlessness, tumult, and madness" (Poteat 1985:4). But as we yearned to be like the gods (but not like the God of Israel, who has never sought to be free from the contingency and unpredictability of history), we gradually lost track of the recipe that lists the basic ingredients of our identity as creatures. In the unrequited search for the foundations of a pure and certain reason untainted by the particularities of custom and convention, the human soul has become a virtual apparition that haunts its body like a ghost. Harold Bloom states that the typically modern self "has found . . . its own freedom — from the world, from time, from other selves. But this freedom is a very expensive torso, because of what it is obliged to leave out: society, temporality, the other. What remains, for it, is solitude and the abyss" (Bloom 1992:37). And we who are the unwitting characters of this story learn more everyday about the erosion of the cohesion and purposefulness that once characterized both history and personal existence.

The modern romancing of divinity exacted a terrible price not only of human beings, but of all creatures whose existence is inextricably interwoven with ours. When we picture ourselves in timeless caprice as lords and masters of the physical world, rather than recognizing our place within it, the rest of creation becomes "something manipulable for the sake of the values we have chosen. It becomes the stock of resources on hand for the fulfillment we value" (Rouse 1987:66). Everything that is "external" to the disembodied human soul is regarded as something to be conquered, possessed, controlled, colonized. We even view our own bodies as property that we own rather than as essentially what we are. Few things in our day and time are more telling than the celebration of the human body, inasmuch as "the 'body' so celebrated turns out to be the body created by the presumption that there is an 'I' that *has* a body" (Hauerwas 1995:24). Although such celebrations may seem like little more than "the narcissistic cultivation of bodily appearance [they are] in fact an expression of a concern lying much deeper actively to 'construct' and control the body" (Giddens 1991:7).

Ironically, the effort to subdue or manage fate by means of a complex technical organization now determines our fate through the very methods, techniques, and institutions that were designed and instituted to depose *Fortuna* from her throne. We have at our disposal immense manipulative powers that reflect values that we have chosen, and yet at the same time these powers and capabilities are embodied in techniques and institutions that in a very real sense have come to possess us. Our understanding of who we are and what is at stake in our lives has increasingly been vested in practices that "are focused by a will to power, a continual striving for increased control and more precise determination of ourselves and the world, that is *never* subordinated to any other concern" (Rouse 1987:261, Rouse's emphasis). Only in recent years, assisted by the keen vision of hindsight, have we discovered to our dismay that few signs remain which indicate that something distinctively human still exists within the world of time and space, save for the overriding concern to maintain the powers of a largely fleeting sovereignty (see Polanyi 1962:380, and Levinas 1989:78).

This is the late modern or postmodern world that the church is called upon by God to engage in creative and redemptive ways. It is also the world that calls into question the continued viability of the type of cultural sponsorship fostered by the ancient regime of Christendom. However, if the church is to embody the grace and mercy of the city that is to come in such a harsh and divisive time as this, it must come to terms with some of its basic structures and tendencies. What follows should not be considered an exhaustive description of these mechanisms, but a brief sketch of some of the more prominent aspects of a world that once prided itself on having come of age, but now increasingly wonders where it all went so askew.

The Inventions of the Universal Man and the Secular World

As noted in the introduction to this book, a prodigious confidence, bordering on arrogance, characterized Descartes and his contemporaries. The pioneers of the modern age did not acknowledge any boundaries to their curiosity, any barriers to their ability to understand the world, any limits to their activities or to their authority. They considered the whole earth to be theirs, and perhaps even the cosmos as well. They proudly asserted that their laws and axioms recapitulated the governing principles of the universe. As far as they were concerned, the earth and all that resided therein constituted, for all intents and purposes, their exclusive domain. The world was theirs to command, and they set out to secure what was clearly (according to the "pure light of reason") their *dominium,* to which they had natural right of ownership.

They further believed that this ambitious program could be carried out while at the same time preserving what Robert Jenson calls the realist faith in a narratable world, a faith that they had inherited from their "unenlightened" forebears. These pioneers of the modern age thus continued to believe in all sincerity

that the world "out there" is such that stories can
be told that are true *to it*. And modernity supposed
that the reason narratives can be true to the world is
that the world somehow "has" its own true story an-
tecedent to, and enabling of, the stories we tell about
ourselves.... Put it this way: the way in which the
modern West has talked about human life supposes
that an omniscient historian could write a *universal*
history, and that this is so because the universe with
inclusion of our lives is in fact a story written by a
sort of omnipotent novelist (Jenson 1993:20).

According to Jenson, there is no mystery about the source
of modernity's faith in a narratable world. It originated in
Jewish and Christian practice, according to which the universe in which the human task and possibility take place
is in fact a story written by a sort of omnipotent novelist:
"The story the Bible tells is asserted to be the story of God
with His creatures; that is, it is both assumed and explicitly
asserted that there is a true story about the universe because
there is a universal novelist/historian" (Jenson 1993:20f).

For centuries it was the job of theology to unpack the
relationship of the world of time and space to the story of
God narrated in Scripture, for apart from this relationship
of finite to infinite, of the created order to its proton and
eschaton, the world and all that dwells therein could not
be rightly understood. To be sure, human knowledge of the
infinite was limited, pursued for the most part under the
apophatic sign (denoting what God is not), but this meant
that our understanding of the finite world, because its beginning and end resided in God, was also limited. But if
there is little doubt as to the source of this faith in a narratable world, says Jenson, neither is there much mystery about

how that faith has been lost in a growing melancholia that currently haunts the offspring of modernity, for it was essentially "defined by the attempt to live in a universal story without a universal storyteller." In short, the project that is the modern world sought to sustain its inherited faith in a narratable world while at the same time withdrawing allegiance from "the God who was that faith's object" (Jenson 1993:21). The understanding of the limits of knowledge, the humility that must accompany the quest for truth, also went by the wayside in this new, brave universe.

A radical redefinition of the concept of the secular therefore lay at the heart of the Cartesian shift.[62] As we noted in the previous chapter, the Latin *saeculum* did not refer to a space or realm separate from the religious or sacred, but to the temporal period between fall and eschaton, and thus to the here and now. And though it is true that the ecclesiastical institutions of Christendom increasingly accommodated themselves to the practices of the present age, the church still thought of itself as the *civitas peregrina,* the city of God whose pilgrimage through this temporal order marked the period of the *saeculum.* According to this account, everything that happens in the realm of time and space — every person, community, and event, every institution, practice, and disposition, every rock and tree and rabbit — finds its place and significance within the narrative framework of biblical protology and eschatology. Within the architectonic framework of this story, the world has both a beginning and an end (in both senses of those terms) that give to everything that happens in between its sense and direction. In spite of its many shortcomings, therefore, the medieval church retained in both structure and piety at least an attenuated sense of a providentially governed history together with its identity as an eschatological city.

In short, although the institutions of Christendom never achieved what their first proponents set out to accomplish — to liberate the present world from the dominion of death and darkness, and make it new before God by the power of the Holy Spirit — neither did they completely abandon the narrative understanding of history inscribed in Israel's poetizing memory and sustained by the practices of both diasporic Judaism and the early church. As John Yoder observes, the "higher level of morality asked of the clergy, the international character of the hierarchy, the visibility of the hierarchy in opposition to the princes, the gradual moral education of barbarians into monogamy and legality, foreign missions, apocalypticism and mysticism — all of these preserved an awareness, however distorted and polluted, of the strangeness of God's people in a rebellious world" (Yoder 1994b:58). The Scripture's eschatological sense of history was forsaken only after a second transformation in ecclesial practice and social polity took place.

The key feature of the first, or Constantinian, shift lay in the gradual eclipse of the church's "spiritual freedom and eschatological identity as the proleptic presence of the new order of Christ's Kingdom" (Guroian 1987:148). This eclipse occurred as the church increasingly bound itself to the world as its spiritual form. The second, or Cartesian, shift jettisoned the eschatological framework of early Christianity altogether, along with the ecclesial practices and relationships that sought (albeit imperfectly) to bind life in the *saeculum* to its beginning and end in the mystery of God's providential design. In place of the biblical story about the overlap of two ages, the leading figures of the Renaissance and the Enlightenment imagined not a time, but a space over which human beings were sovereign. The architects of the Cartesian shift decided that if humans were ever to make this "natural" sovereignty a reality, they had to be set free from the constraints of local communities and eventually from what was considered to be a dubious and altogether extraneous working hypothesis called "God." The idea of the secular came to refer to this carefully demarcated sphere of action that supposedly contained and ordered (both practically and theoretically) all finite entities and events in isolation from any relationship to the infinite.

Although they did not recognize it at the time, we now know that Descartes and his contemporaries did not discover the clear and indubitable principles of reason's "natural light" upon which all other inquiry could be safely grounded.[63] Instead, they substituted new working hypotheses for prior assumptions about God, the human being, and the world as the basis of their operations, and their speculative conceits were inscribed into the new order of things. The new definition of the secular was perhaps the single most important of these new suppositions. A second postulate followed on the heels of the first, and was quickly woven into the social and intellectual fabric of modernity. It consisted of a set of reciprocal images, analogies, and attitudes that converged into a picture of a self unfettered by the physical body or the webs of interlocution embedded in social and geographical ties. This picture of an unencumbered self was declared to be the universal man [sic] who, although he may or may not be affected by what happens in his particular spot in history and society, was nonetheless "capable of cutting himself loose from the communal roots and loyalties; of lifting himself, so to speak, onto a higher plane and taking from there a long, detached and critical view of communal demands and pressures" (Bauman 1993:39). It was this universal man, or "thinking thing," that was expected to exercise absolute dominion over the space of the secular.

The attractions of the Enlightenment picture of the human person are not hard to imagine. The sense of freedom posited by the practical suppositions of the universal man, namely, "the right (and skill) to fashion oneself," was intoxicating. "Suddenly," says Zygmunt Bauman, "one's fate — only yesterday bewailed for its tyranny or grudgingly surrendered to for the same reason — appeared to be pliable in the hands of the self-conscious man as clay was in the palms of a skillful sculptor." The prospect of escaping the reach of fate was eagerly embraced, for it in effect promised human beings that they would no longer be "cast into immutable shape by the accident of birth, nor kept on a short string by the small parcel of humanity to which they happened to be assigned" (Bauman 1993:22f). In a very real sense the Cartesian shift represented a concerted effort to divorce human identity from all forms of historical and social entanglements, which by their very nature are always tied to particular times and places.

According to this picture, human beings could set themselves over against the rest of the created order in much the same way that Judaism and Christianity had traditionally conceived of God's relationship to a world created *ex nihilo,* out of nothing. This amazing, but heretofore unknown, ability coincided harmoniously with the desire of many in "polite society" (that is to say, the powerful) to distance themselves from "the motley collection of parishioners, kinsmen and other locals." The postulate of the universal man "squared well with the uniforming ambitions and practices of the modern state, with the war it declared on *les pouvoirs intermédiaires,* with its cultural crusades against local customs redefined as superstitions and condemned to death for the crime of resisting central-ized management" (Bauman 1993:39). This depiction of the universal man again stands in stark contrast with both the Jewish and Christian traditions, according to which human beings exist *as human* only within contingent webs of interlocution that ultimately begin and end with God.

Although this new secular realm and its goal of a heaven on earth began to take concrete shape during the seventeenth-century European Enlightenment, Renaissance humanists were the first to speculate about such a world. Theologians led the way by removing theological concerns from the arena of ecclesial practice, where they attended to the relationship of the triune God to a fallen and redeemed creation, and turning them into elements in a philosophical debate about the intelligibility and coherence of "theism" versus "deism."[64] This reconceptualization of theological discourse unwittingly stimulated the humanists' dream of putting "man at the centre of the universe, to deify him" (Carroll 1993:preface). Their overarching ambition, writes Bauman, "was nothing less than to found an entirely human order on earth, and one that would be erected entirely with the help of human capacities and resources alone" (Bauman 1993:23).[65] The liberation of humankind, or at least some part of it, from the unpredictable power of fate and *Fortuna* was squarely at the heart of the aspirations of the Renais-sance. It was this seductive vision of an area of sheer human autonomy that the leading lights of the Enlightenment in both Europe and America set out to make a reality.[66]

The dramatic vision of an entirely human order on earth, erected solely with human capacities and resources, served implicitly to narrate the story of the everyday world without reference to the God who had previously been its prem-ise and principal character. It is fundamentally misleading, however, to see the history of ideas developing independent of the history of political and economic change, or to make one prior to or dependent on the other. The shift from biblical depictions of the world to modern conceptions of an autonomous secular realm did not take place in the abstract, nor did it represent the unfolding of a nonexistent foundational reason. It occurred rather in conjunction with the rise of such social institutions as the nation-state and capitalist relations of production and consumption. Theory and practice are therefore bound to each other in a seamless whole. Theory is a mode of action that explicates a particular sociohistorical practice. Such practices, conversely, are never mindless, but incorporate ideas and images that render explicit their goals, means, and supporting institutions, thus opening them to both internal and external scrutiny.

The theoretical pioneers of the Enlightenment — Descartes, Francis Bacon, Hugo Grotius, Thomas Hobbes, Baruch de Spinoza, just to mention a few of the more prominent names — labored diligently in virtually every field of endeavor to sever the workings of the finite or natural world from any direct involvement in or meaningful reference to the (supernatural) mystery of divine providence. Their labors, moreover, were not limited to the subjugation of what we now think of as nature.[67] The new sciences of political science, political economy, and sociology not only posited the existence of a secular human realm purged of any religious residue, but also claimed that this new object of inquiry was a field of power and knowledge governed by invariable laws that could be known *etsi Deus non daretur.*[68] To be sure, these first social scientists thought about this purely human domain in a number of different ways. Grotius and Hobbes, for example, thought that the political realm was strictly a human construct, whereas political economists such as Adam Smith and James Stewart reintroduced the notion of an overarching process into the operations of the market that coordinated in quasi-providential fashion the self-interested activities of individual human wills. Sociology, dominated by such noted figures as Auguste Comte and Max Weber, reversed this relationship, positing "a social *système* which preceded any politics and *prise de conscience* on the part of individuals; a set of social facts and laws *prior* to virtue and prior to the setting of goals for action" (Milbank 1990:53). Nevertheless, all shared the common goal of removing what they regarded as the purely human space of the *saeculum* from the effective reach of that love which moves the sun and the other stars.

Those who sought to separate the world of time and space from the orbit of divine providence gained a most important ally in the German philosopher Immanuel Kant.[69] Kant's primary goal was to specify once and for all the range and limits of human knowledge formerly set by the tension between finite and infinite, but now with reference to the universal man. He managed to convince several generations of scholars that it was possible (assuming the absolute veracity of Newtonian physics and the moral sagacity of Lutheran piety) to isolate and exhaustively catalogue the categories of pure understanding that define and order the essential, lawlike properties of both the natural and social worlds. Of course, once the scope of Newtonian physics and the validity of Lutheran piety become problematic, as they eventually did, the ability of "pure reason" to round off the limits of finitude is also called into question. "No sooner does one discover the categories of pure understanding for a Newtonian age," Richard Rorty observes, than somebody draws up another list that would do nicely for an Aristotelian or an Einsteinian one. No sooner does one draw up a categorical imperative for Christians than somebody draws up one which works for cannibals. No sooner does one develop an evolutionary epistemology which explains why our science is so good than somebody writes a science-fiction story about bug-eyed and monstrous evolutionary epistemologists praising bug-eyed and monstrous scientists for the survival value of their monstrous theories (Rorty 1982:167f).

Kant's way of rounding off finitude, moreover, also guaranteed that the categories of "pure reason" did not extend directly to the "transcendent realm." He did of course leave open the possibility of human access to the infinite, but only as a derivative inference of practical reason, which was grounded in the new (and, as it turns out, quite problematic) conception of human freedom. This bifurcation of reason had the chilling effect of relegating so-called religious matters, as Dietrich Bonhoeffer puts it, "to a realm beyond the world of experience" (Bonhoeffer 1971:341). In other words, Kant claimed not only to have grasped the true nature of the physical universe as rational creatures perceive it, but at the same time protected all that properly belongs to the sphere of human freedom, including religious beliefs. This "protection," however, effectively removed ecclesial practices and convictions from any kind of involvement in the public domain of the everyday world, and put them at the margins of life, where our capacity to quantify, predict, and control the phenomenal world gives out.[70] As the later history of the church amply demonstrates, this was a very high cost to pay for protection.

What the pioneers of the secular age finally concocted was a social regime of power and knowledge that even in a postmodern context continues to exercise "immense tutelary power" (de Tocqueville 1981:385, as cited by Taylor 1991:9). Of course, concoction is not the word they would have used to describe the matter, for they were convinced that the secular realm was a given. They insisted, moreover, that this domain had always existed, though for much of human history our ability to acknowledge this reality lay dormant, hidden under what sociologist Peter Berger would later describe as a "sacred canopy" of ancient myths and medieval metaphysics (Berger 1967). In other words, they simply assumed that religion had for centuries hidden the true nature of the world from humanity, and only in this, the age of science, had they been able to poke holes in this canopy and see what the universe is really like. The realm of the secular only needed to be disentangled from the silly sagas and overwrought speculations of our unenlightened forebears and allowed to shine forth through the barrier that had once hidden it from view. Some even argued that this desacralizing tendency could be located at the origins of Christianity, but it was suppressed by the imperial aspirations of ecclesiastical institutions during the Constantinian era. According to this version of the story, modern theologians, in collaboration with the new science of sociology, finally succeeded in stripping away the irrational husk of ecclesial restrictions to reveal the purity of humankind's spiritual kernel. And they did indeed free spirituality from any public interference, precisely by removing it from any meaningful involvement in the public sphere (the classic example is, of course, von Harnack 1957).

Fortune, Risk, and the Empty Self

Bonhoeffer, in a brief outline to a book that he would never get the chance to write, offers a very different picture of the secular domain from that sketched by proponents of the modern regime. He states that in the first chapter he would deal with the emergence of the modern world as the self-proclaimed "coming of age of humankind." Foremost among the concerns of this age was the

> safeguarding of life against "accidents" and "blows of fate"; even if these cannot be eliminated, the danger can be reduced. Insurance (which, although it lives on "accidents," seeks to mitigate their effects) is a western phenomenon. The aim: to be independent of nature. Nature was formerly conquered by spiritual means, with us by technical organization of all kinds. Our immediate environment is not nature, as formerly, but organization. But with this protection from nature's menace there arises a new one — through organization itself (Bonhoeffer 1971:380).

Bonhoeffer clearly does not regard the modern secular domain as a given that only needs to be unveiled by the "pure reason" first identified by modern philosophers and then employed by scientists, politicians, and businessmen. It is instead a complex technical edifice that a particular group of human beings (most of whom came originally from northern Europe) constructed over the last three centuries or so in an attempt to guard against the intrusions of fortune into human affairs. From this standpoint the domain of the secular is not something that was previously obscured from view by a sacerdotal tent, erected by conspiratorial priests intent on consolidating an illicit authority over us.

Rather, it more closely resembles the interior space of a building that has been subdivided by movable partitions. The overriding purpose of this subdivision is to efficiently contain, survey, and supervise what goes on within this space. In short, the new secular realm has been fashioned rather than found. It was literally created by means of practices, social roles, equipment, and goals, the aim of which is to control and predict with ever-increasing precision all that falls within its technical regime.

It is this vast technical organization that sets modern (and now postmodern) existence apart from all other forms of human life. The everyday activities of most people are no longer attuned to the rhythms of nature, the changing of the seasons, the patterns of other life forms, the peculiarities of particular places and times, or the institutions, crafts, and habits that once mediated human interaction with the rest of creation. An immense variety of artifacts, techniques, and disciplines that embody immense manipulative powers over large sectors of nature has replaced such things. The determination of who we are and what is at stake in our lives has been increasingly vested in this technical regime. In particular, the variety of choices we value so highly in a liberal society is a function of the technical environment that closely monitors and supervises our every move. What is regularly held up as the hallmark of our freedom — the vast range of choices that we enjoy — has ironically become the means of our subjection.

Bonhoeffer also draws our attention to the aspiration of modern human beings to eliminate (or at least mitigate) the role that fate plays in their lives. In virtually every other epoch of history, freedom and fate were seen as interlacing threads in the delicate weave of the fabric that is creaturely life. In the heroic sagas of the ancient world, the thought of classical antiquity, the many volumes of medieval Christian, Jewish, and Islamic theology, and even in the writings of such Renaissance figures as Machiavelli it was understood that one could resist, and perhaps for a time even surmount, fortune, but that eventually it would win out. Only those who knew how to respond appropriately to fate — regardless of whether one thought that it was indifferent to human suffering or ultimately subject to some form of comprehensive design — were truly moral, truly happy, truly free. In the Christian tradition, for example, the seemingly whimsical turns of fortune were tied to the acknowledgment of life as donation. Freedom was a gift to be enjoyed in praise and love of God who orders all things. The unpredictability of fate was a sign of the pervasiveness and persistence of original sin within the present age, but this sign did not exist in isolation, but was dramatically located within an overarching providential design.[71] All told, prior to the rise of the modern world few people really thought they could be more than the coauthor of their own stories. They understood that human beings subsisted in a complex web of interlocking narratives under the guiding hand of *Fortuna* (MacIntyre 1984:199).

In the modern era, in contrast, freedom (which according to the postulate of the universal man is simply the abstract ability to choose) and fate have been defined as mutually exclusive. In a very real and important sense the goal of the modern project was to make it possible for human beings to write their own life stories without interference from anyone or anything else. People could finally take destiny solely into their own hands and fashion a protective shield around themselves and their private concerns, for example, their business or their immediate family. The institutions of state, market, and civil society have but one ultimate and unifying purpose in such a setting — to ensure that individuals have access to the resources they need to pursue their self-chosen conceptions of the good life free from the uninvited influence of others. A community is, from this standpoint, little more than "the co-existence of (at best) mutually tangential projects" (Williams 1995:4).

The Enlightenment sought the means for overcoming fate primarily in a distinctive form of reflexivity, that is, in a way of acting and thinking about the world that differed substantially from that of their forebears. Prior to Descartes, knowledge about the world and the human condition was generated and passed on within and between communities in the form of tradition. A tradition is not, as it is often caricatured, a dogmatic set of beliefs handed down virtually unchanged from generation to generation, but the practices and institutions that sustain the ongoing deliberations of a community about the type of goods it should pursue and how these goods should be ordered and distributed. The never-ending series of recollections, repetitions, expectations, and resolutions that constitute a tradition are therefore intrinsic to the way in which a particular group of people learn to reason about themselves and the world they inhabit.

In contrast, the pioneers of the modern world, in their quest to conquer fate, believed they needed to acquire this knowledge apart from the constraints of any and all tradition. To this end they sought rational procedures and epistemic standards that were independent of what any group of people happened to think and do in a particular time and place. In the search for these universal standards, the "original progenitors of modern science and philosophy believed themselves to be preparing the way for securely founded knowledge of the social and natural worlds: the claims of reason were due to overcome the dogmas of tradition, offering a sense of certitude in place of the arbitrary character of habit and custom" (Giddens 1991:21). In what turned out to be a rhetorical ploy, they set the clarity of "reason" over against the obfuscation of "tradition." Descartes sought this kind of knowledge through a program of radical doubt, believing that he could weed out all false claims to our assent. When he came to that belief or set of beliefs that was self-evident and thus could not be reasonably doubted, he would have discovered a solid foundation for adjudicating all other assertions to truth. The world would then have the single and compelling authority that it desperately needed. Later generations of scholars found serious errors in Descartes' arguments, but these did not lead them to abandon his project. They decided instead that they only needed to tinker with the way he set it up.

The irony that overshadows the Cartesian search for a method that would provide certainty in a world of contingency comes to the fore precisely at this point. As Giddens notes, "the reflexivity of modernity turns out to confound the expectations of Enlightenment thought — although it is the very product of that thought." Put simply, Descartes' methodological principle of radical doubt effectively undermines any and all claims to certainty. This subversion of reason as the quest for indubitable knowledge did not stay confined to the philosophy seminar room, but "permeates into everyday life as well as philosophical consciousness, and forms a general existential dimension of the contemporary social world. Modernity institutionalises the principle of radical doubt and insists that all knowledge takes the form of hypotheses: claims which may very well be true, but which are in principle always open to revision and may have at some point to be abandoned" (Giddens 1991:21,

3). Unfortunately, we could never be sure whether we even formulated our hypotheses correctly, because any criteria we draw up to make that determination would be subject to the same kind of radical doubt. The standards by which modern reflexivity is judged obviously do not reside in theory alone, but in a very distinctive form of social practice.

If the methods and techniques that underwrote the Enlightenment quest for certainty, and that continue to shape and direct everyday life in spite of their failure to make good on their promises, were truly the deliverances of reason's "natural light," then we would be forced to conclude that reason is a cruel tempter, more capricious than any of the gods of antiquity. Indeed, as Johann Georg Hamann observed a century before Friedrich Nietzsche began his assault on the pretensions of the modern age, the Enlightenment devotion to a hypostasized reason is in actuality a throwback to pagan divination: "The object of your reflections and devotion is not God, but a mere word-image, like your universal human reason, which by a more than poetic license you deify as a real person, making so many similar gods and persons by the transubstantiation [sic] of your word-images that the grossest heathendom and blindest popery in comparison to your philosophical idolatry will be justified and perhaps acquitted on the day of judgment" (Hamann, as cited in Smith 1960:204).

For our purposes, however, a more useful way to decipher the reflexive techniques that flow from the Enlightenment quest for certainty is to expand upon Bonhoeffer's description of them as components in a distinctive practical regime. This "technical organization of all kinds," as he puts it, is not a given, but a specific type of social performance that projects its own distinctive (if implicit) webs of interlocution. It turns out that the postmodern body politic is no less determinative of self-identity than previous societies were. The overall pattern has changed dramatically in many ways, to be sure, but the same kind of interpellative social dynamic is at work. Although most people no longer see the formation of their self-identity in connection with the particularities of their social groupings, who they are and what they do are still in fact the products of political, economic, and cultural mechanisms that neatly confine the apparent diversity of lifestyles within the architectonic structures of contemporary society.

According to the script of this social drama, secular human beings have little choice but to be "individuals."[72] This does not mean, however, that personal identity flows spontaneously from the springs of pure autonomy within the universal man. It means rather that "the self, like the broader institutional contexts in which it exists, has to be reflexively made." Self-identity in the late modern age is thus constructed "in the context of multiple choice as filtered through abstract systems" (Giddens 1991:5f).[73] These choices, moreover, are carefully coordinated by overlapping mechanisms of social control. In short, not only do we have little choice but to be individuals in this society; we are also condemned to realize our individuality preeminently as consumers. Lifestyle choice is for the most part unavoidable, not simply for affluent groups or classes, but also for those who struggle to get by under conditions of severe material constraint.[74]

Kathleen Norris, in the course of a delightful exploration of the monastic vocation, is therefore on target when she asserts that the modern idol of the autonomous individual, which supposedly rules out of bounds any purpose beyond one's self, is in fact a sham: "The truth is we expect everyone to be the same, and dismiss as elitist those who are working through a call to any genuine vocation."[75] Rather than call it a sham, however, I suggest that we think of the idea of the autonomous individual as a character in a dramatic work of fiction (in the literal sense of these terms). The reflexive habits and categories that make up the technical organization of modernity and postmodernity serve to enact this very distinctive drama on the stage of history. The webs of interlocution embedded in this apparatus take concrete form as a reflexive project, at the heart of which is this peculiar character in the postmodern drama.

As a consequence of this dramatic production, each of us "not only 'has,' but *lives* a biography reflexively organised in terms of flows of social and psychological information about possible ways of life" (Giddens 1991:14). The paradox of human beings under the conditions of modernity, having little or no choice but to choose who and what they will be as individuals, is thoroughgoing: as traditional ways of life lose their hold and the daily business of life is reconstituted in terms of the technical organization of modernity, persons are increasingly required to negotiate lifestyle choices among a diversity of options. This pluralism of lifestyles is, however, strictly confined to the private level, for the ultimate good is predetermined by the institutional regime of the secular world. This regime institutes and enforces a particular (if deliberately tacit) moral hierarchy: the role of the market as sole manager of the heterogeneity of interests, the superlative value of scientific progress, the sovereignty of choice itself (Giddens 1991:1, 5; Cavanaugh 1995:409).

What is unique about the Enlightenment construct of the individual is therefore not simply its reflexive accumulation of knowledge about human life as the basis on which choices are made. All human beings, in one form or another, have routinely "kept in touch" with the grounds of what they do as an integral element of doing it. But as I noted above, keeping in touch through the acquisition of knowledge with what a community and its members do has historically been the responsibility of those institutions and practices that constitute a tradition. The conversations and debates that pervade, organize, and monitor the activities of this community do not necessarily resist change. Rather, they take their bearings from a set of "temporal and spatial markers in terms of which change can have any meaningful form" (Giddens 1990:37). Reflexivity in the form of a tradition allows a community over time to discover and name the goods that, as they pursue them, make them who and what they are.

With the rise of the modern world, however, reflexivity takes on a radically new and different character. Human reason is no longer defined as an attribute of the many practices that fund our common participation in the world of time and space, for which particular sets of concepts are but the temporary cross sections (Toulmin 1972:133). It is depicted instead as a quasi-divine power that in many and diverse ways actually *configures* the world, both theoretically and practically, around the fictional character of the individual. Everyday life is constituted by the roles this character plays within the reflexive organization of knowledge environments or, as Bonhoeffer refers to them, technical organization of all kinds (Giddens 1990:36–39). Modern reflexivity thus ushered the world across a critical threshold where, as Michel Foucault puts it, "the formation of knowledge and the increase of power regularly reinforce one another in a circular process" (Foucault 1977:224). Self-identity is therefore cultivated, not in explicit connection with the distinctive traits of traditional social groupings, but within technical environments and organized around "individuals."

Who somebody is and what he or she does are no longer matters that are set within the explicit harmonies of an intentional community. Personal identity must now be constructed within the vast (though often implicit) technical organization of modernity. The disciplines that make up this organization reconstitute daily life as part of the reflexive project of the individual. These disciplines, or as Giddens refers to them, "disembedding mechanisms," are institutional processes that uproot social relationships and identities that were once embedded in local contexts, and redistribute them across vast distances in time and space. He divides these mechanisms into two types. The first are symbolic tokens, which he defines as "media of interchange which can be 'passed around' without regard to the specific characteristics of individuals or groups that handle them at any particular juncture." Although Giddens cites money as the preeminent symbolic token of modernity, perhaps the prototype of all secular symbolic tokens was citizenship in the nation-state. This way of linking political association and personal identity, unique to the modern world and another of its working hypotheses, shifted political authority and allegiance away from particular social relationships and toward an abstract entity within an often arbitrarily defined territory (Giddens 1990:22–27).

The spread of expert systems throughout the technical regime of modernity represents the other type of disembedding mechanism that tears everyday life away from local affiliations. Expert systems are networks of technical or professional expertise that continuously organize ever-expanding areas of our daily existence, but apart from any kind of deliberation regarding the ends pursued. Like symbolic tokens, these systems remove social relations from the immediacies of moral contexts and reconfigure them within carefully delineated knowledge environments. Most of us know little or nothing about the codes of knowledge used by architects, economists, engineers, physicians, therapists, and so forth and yet every day in countless ways we have little choice but to place our faith in what they do. The role that technology plays in organizing modern society, which is widely acknowledged, would not be possible except for these expert systems whose influence often goes unnoticed. Every time we ride in a car, enroll in a health maintenance organization, arrange for a mortgage to buy a house, or log onto the Internet, we not only involve ourselves more deeply in overlapping systems of expertise, but we also entrust them with determining the meaning of larger and larger chunks of our existence. Taken separately, the degree of trust expended may seem inconsequential, but when we begin to contemplate what our lives would be like without the whole complex of these systems, the resulting sense of disorientation can be overwhelming (Giddens 1990:27–29).

The importance of expert systems is not limited to those aspects of modern life where complex technology is involved. Endeavors that once were the venue of local communities, such as raising children, have also been subsumed by interlocking systems of expertise. For example, it is a commonplace in popular culture to recite the African proverb that it takes a village to raise a child. At one time among the most common form of political community, the village is particularly well-suited for sustaining the face-to-face affiliations of local societies. Villages are invariably made up by an odd assortment of characters known as neighbors who help parents care for their children. To be sure, the line between helping and meddling is often blurred, but the kinds of people that inhabit real villages, if they are to care enough to help, must "also have the power — indeed, they would say, the responsibility — to chasten, to correct, to chastise" (Elshtain 1996:33).[76] This power and responsibility is tied to the fact that in this kind of political association the task of raising children is not left entirely to the discretion of individual parents, but is governed by the explicit goal of initiating the next generation into a particular form of life, with specific goods that are not subject to individual choice. Self-identity is thus cultivated in keeping with the social ethos of the village.

But whereas it once took a village to raise a child, it now seems to require a vast network of professionals.[77] In place of the pedagogical goals of the village and the assistance of imperfect neighbors, we have an army of educational, financial, legal, medical, psychological, and social work experts whose job it is to manage the next generation of individuals. The triumph of expert systems can also be seen in the areas of politics, religion, and law enforcement, where the idioms of therapeutic and managerial competence increasingly dominate, but again without reference to or conversation about the goals that people ought to pursue in common. The eclipse of traditional goods and virtues that occurs as these systems of expertise assume control over virtually every aspect our lives, and as a consequence of the faith we place, wittingly or not, in their technical know-how, has resulted in an atrophying sense of how to make substantive moral judgments. Indeed, the basic skills that are required to make these kinds of judgments are rapidly becoming a lost art form (quick, call in the experts who specialize in teaching "life skills!").

The inhabitants of postmodern culture, with few exceptions, must now undertake the reflexive task of constructing their individual self-identities on their own, each choosing her or his own conception of the good life, but without the benefit of reliable moral landmarks or guides to lead them through the process. Contrary to the expectations of the Enlightenment, these practical and theoretical guideposts are not supplied by the phantom of "pure reason," and traditional markers have for the most part eroded under the force of secular reflexivity. Human beings have been systematically separated from the moral resources necessary to live meaningful and satisfying lives. In short, although the reflexive project of the self generates impressive programs of actualization and mastery, "as long as these possibilities are understood largely as a matter of the extension of the control systems of modernity to the self, they lack moral meaning." This project thus constitutes "both a pre-eminent value and a framework for self-actualisation, but represents a morally stunted process" (Giddens 1991:9).

We should have the wisdom and courage to admit that the Enlightenment quest for certainty did not lead to the type of scientifically managed control over nature and society that its advocates sought. Instead, the desire to be like the gods has given rise to a way of life quite different from what was envisioned at the outset. Giddens refers to this pattern of social life in late modernity as a risk culture. He does not mean by this that social life is intrinsically more dangerous than it once was. For most people in the developed areas of the world this is simply not the case, fears about the dangers of modern urban and suburban life (often exaggerated by sensational reports in the media) notwithstanding. It is rather to indicate, in contrast to other times and places, that the calculation of risk is now central to the way that individuals — lay actors and technical specialists alike — reflexively cope with the world they inhabit (Giddens 1991:3).

Constituted as individuals within the post-traditional order of modernity, human beings now have little choice but to try to gain control over their identities "by means of the reflexive organisation of knowledge environments." To exist as an individual, therefore, is to imagine yourself essentially separate from the world of space and time so that you can treat the future as a "territory, as it were, [to be] carved out and colonised" (Giddens 1991:3f).[78] Individuals strive to overcome the arbitrary influence of fate by treating everyone and everything else they encounter as objects situated within a space that can be minutely organized and managed. The objects that make up this environment are seen either as threats to, or opportunities for the realization of, the reflexive project of the self as an individual.[79] One's ability to colonize the future is never absolute, and thus "thinking in terms of risk is vital to assessing how far projects are likely to diverge from their anticipated outcomes. Risk assessment invites precision, and even quantification, but by its nature is imperfect" (Giddens 1991:3f).[80] Moreover, the inherent moral paradox of a risk culture is that we find ourselves "involved in a world in which we are simultaneously trying to render the rest of society predictable and ourselves unpredictable, to devise generalizations which will capture the behavior of others and to cast our own behavior into forms which will elude the generalizations which others frame" (MacIntyre 1984:104).

The technical mechanisms of modern culture replace all tradition-based engagements with *Fortuna* with the calculation of risk, and thus bring about "an alteration in the perception of determination and contingency, such that human moral imperatives, natural causes, and chance reign in place of religious cosmologies" (Giddens 1990:34). The reflexive organization of the self around knowledge environments (which have become more and more commercialized in recent decades) shoves to the periphery the institutions and practices, habits and relationships that underwrote inherited notions of providence, fortune, destiny, and fate. The uprooting of personal identity from the daily activities, habits, and allegiances of church, mosque, synagogue, and temple effectively prevents these communities and their intellectual and moral traditions from interfering with the public sphere of power and knowledge — politics, law, economics, and science — that have been reserved solely for the institutions of the modern secular domain.[81]

Whither the Sweet Dream of Reason?

The modern quest of the "universal man" and the promotion of a risk culture did not result in the general increase of freedom and human flourishing envisioned by the leading figures of the Renaissance and Enlightenment. We have belatedly discovered that human beings do not innately possess (as one of the working hypotheses of the Enlightenment led us to believe) a timeless inner core that provides every individual with an unquenchable source of reason and value, a sure foundation for his or her actions and affections. Simply put, there is no universal man. Women and men are rather, as Rorty puts it, "historical all the way through" (Rorty 1988:258). As a consequence, when the technical regime of modernity began to separate systematically the formation of personal identity — practically and theoretically — from the local face-to-face associations that locate this process within a shared reservoir of meaning, it also, most unwittingly, drained the self of its moral, spiritual, and intellectual content as well.

The Renaissance dream of a heaven on earth thus set in motion a series of events that was intended to liberate human beings from all external constraints, but instead it cut them loose from communal roots and traditions, and also from the habits and customs that bound them to the earth. Moral agency was sundered from meaningful points of reference beyond individual wants and desires. The loss of any purpose or goal beyond the self in turn emptied it of substantive social content. The price human beings pay for this contentless, directionless liberation has been devastating. This empty self of the modern age, says Philip Cushman, desperately tries to compensate for what it has lost by seeking "the experience of being continually filled up by consuming goods, calories, experiences, politicians, romantic partners, and empathic therapists in an attempt to combat the growing alienation and fragmentation of its era" (Cushman 1990:600).

Moreover, says Cushman, in addition to its obvious spiritual, moral, and ecological poverty, the political significance of the empty self is immense. The state does not need to resort continually to the threat of overt coercion to manage the behavior of its citizens. Neither does it need to try to restrict their impulses, as was attempted during the Victorian era. Instead, says Cushman, it has largely accomplished this goal "by creating and manipulating their wish to be soothed, organized, and made cohesive by momentarily filling them up. The products of the social sciences, and of psychology in particular, have often worked to the advantage of the state by helping to construct selves that are the subjects of control and to develop techniques that are the means of control" (Cushman 1990:600; see also Cushman 1995). Like drug addicts, postmodern individuals are hooked on what only a risk culture can provide.

Due to the emptiness of the postmodern subject, "spirituality" has an important role to play in the technical organization of a risk culture. The goals of spirituality in this culture are very different, however, from those that informed the mission and piety of the early church. When Descartes and his contemporaries set out to make the working hypothesis of a secular domain a reality, they also invented the realm of religion, another postulate of modernity that did not exist before the fifteenth century. Prior to the rise of the modern world no one used this term to speak either about a universal impulse embedded in human consciousness, or about beliefs held privately by individuals with no direct bearing on their public lives. When *religio* occurs in medieval writings (which is rare) it usually refers to monastic life, and on occasion to an acquired virtue that — in concert with other virtues — directs the faithful to know and love God. Either way, the term presupposed a context of ecclesial practices embodied in the communal life of the church.

We first encounter the modern idea of religion in Renaissance and Enlightenment texts, where it refers to a freestanding set of beliefs or propositions held by individuals about what is ultimately true and important in life, and, of most importance, which they can hold apart from their political loyalties to another innovation of the period, namely, the rise of the modern state. The plural "religions," a use of the term that would have been unintelligible during the Middle Ages, also appeared at this time as a way to catalogue and thus manage a specific range of concrete practices, goods, and dispositions.[82] In either case, the Enlightenment notions of religion and religions enforce the technical separation of life into two distinct spheres, with the public realm reserved exclusively for the institutional mechanisms of secular culture.

This understanding of "religion" fits very nicely within a postmodern risk culture. The individual in the role of consumer is encouraged to pick and choose from a vast inventory of religious symbols and doctrines, to select those beliefs that best express his or her private sentiments. There are, nevertheless, definite limits to what the individual may choose. At the very least, his or her selection must not conflict with (and ideally should promote) the civil requirements of the state, which in the secular world bears all of the responsibility for arbitrating between competing interests. Noted political columnist George Will observes in this regard that "a central purpose of America's political arrangements is the subordination of religion to the political order, meaning the primacy of democracy. The founders ...wished to tame and domesticate religious passions of the sort that convulsed Europe. They aimed to do so not by establishing religion, but by establishing a commercial republic — capitalism. They aimed to submerge people's turbulent energies in self-interested pursuit of material comforts" (Will, as cited in Hauerwas 1991:30).[83]

As with other areas of contemporary life, postmodern spirituality is characterized by the triumph of the therapeutic mindset (see Rieff's [1967] pioneering work). The term itself has become synonymous with self-care manuals and twelve-step programs, yet another product or service marketed as an effective way to cope with the stress of modern life, overcome substance abuse, move in emotional harmony with the universe, cure disease, or enhance self-esteem. Such spirituality does not require any form of communal direction or oversight, but may be enjoyed in the privacy of your own home, head, and heart. In effect, the Cartesian project transformed Christian piety into a kind of personalized "diet plan" for the soul, complete with "before" and "after" testimonies. This peculiar kind of religiosity, with its decidedly therapeutic orientation, is energetically distributed within the marketplace of desire and eagerly lapped up by countless multitudes. As such, it fits perfectly into the technical organization of secular life and its "disenchantment" of the world.[84]

In many ways the spirituality that prevails in a risk culture more closely resembles ancient Gnosticism than early Christianity. According to Harold Bloom, the dominant form of religion in North America "masks itself as Protestant Christianity yet has ceased to be Christian." Pentecostals, Baptists, Methodists, Presbyterians, and others (including Roman Catholics) may therefore "call themselves Christians, but like most Americans they are closer to ancient Gnostics than to early Christians." This gnosticized form of Christianity has for the most part kept the figure of Jesus, but it is "a very solitary and personal American Jesus, who is also the resurrected Jesus rather than the crucified Jesus or the Jesus who ascended again to the Father." Bloom concludes that although Americans are members of "a religiously mad culture, furiously searching for the spirit," it is also the case that "each of us is subject and object of the one quest, which must be for the original self, a spark of breath in us that we are convinced goes back to before the Creation" (Bloom 1992:22, 32).[85]

The therapeutic allure of Gnosticism is in many ways understandable, because a risk culture, by its very nature, obliterates any meaningful distinction between coercive and noncoercive social relations. The social world has become "nothing but a meeting place for individual wills, each with its own set of attitudes and preferences and who understand that world solely as an arena for the achievement of their own satisfaction, who interpret reality as a series of opportunities for their enjoyment and for whom the last enemy is boredom." In this setting everybody is taught to value his or her identity as an autonomous individual above all else, and so each should aspire not to be manipulated by others. But at the same time, if all of us attempt "to incarnate our own principles and stand-point in the world of practice, we find no way open to us to do so except by directing towards others those very manipulative modes of relationship which each of aspires to resist in our own case" (MacIntyre 1984:25, 68). The implicit assumption of an original, foundational opposition thus underwrites the social order of a secular world.

In such circumstances, the refuge proffered by Gnosticism, which "in the last analysis," says Philip Lee, "is an attempt to escape from everything except the self" (Lee 1987:9f), is quite tempting. It may well be the best way the isolated and empty individual can reconcile herself or himself with an empty social sphere, but it also eliminates any challenge to that sphere's authority. Contemporary Gnosticism, in both Christian and post-Christian forms, represents the Cartesian successor to traditional Christianity in a distinctively secular (that is to say, commercialized) version of Constantinianism. But in this situation, says Bonhoeffer, the question that now confronts us is: "What protects us against the menace of organization? Man is again thrown back on himself. He has managed to deal with everything, only not with himself. He can insure against everything, only not against man. In the last resort it all turns on man." Gnostic spirituality completely lacks the "spiritual force" needed to deal critically and creatively with the postmodern risk culture (Bonhoeffer 1971:341).

When we examine the secular realm closely, we are forced to conclude with Jenson that the modern world pursued its vision of a heaven on earth financed with "moral and intellectual capital that it has not renewed, and indeed could not have renewed without denying itself" (Jenson 1993:20). Now, three and a half centuries later, that world stands precariously on the brink of what Bonhoeffer calls the void. The dominion of this "supreme manifestation of all the powers which are opposed to God" is absolute, engulfing life, history, family, nation, language, faith. The void spares nothing, blowing "its anti-god breath into the nostrils of all that is established and awakens it to a false semblance of new life while sucking out from it its proper essence, until at last it falls in ruin as a lifeless husk and is cast away." It consigns the past to oblivion and conceives of the future as little more than a domain to be conquered and colonized. As a result, says Bonhoeffer,

> there is no longer any meaning in the question of the historical inheritance which requires of those who receive it that they shall both develop it in the present and hand it on to the future. There is no future and there is no past. There is only the moment which has been rescued from the void, and the desire to snatch from the void the next moment as well. . . . Nothing makes a permanent impression and nothing imposes a lasting obligation (Bonhoeffer 1955:105f).

Modern society delayed for a time the dehumanizing effects of a risk culture by selectively drawing on a residual stock of concepts, convictions, practices, and virtues from the traditions of medieval Christendom to underwrite its emancipatory designs. These residual "values" can be seen in the moral philosophies of Descartes, Bentham, Hume, Locke, Kant, and Kierkegaard (just to mention a few), which in their own ways are quite conservative. But as the contents of this residue were separated from their source in an explicit set of ecclesial practices and exposed to the full force of secular reflexivity, they began to erode, somewhat slowly at first, and then more rapidly as the modern era progressed. This process of moral erosion finally discloses contemporary risk culture as "a parasitic form of social arrangement which may stop its parasitic action only when the host organism is sucked dry of its life juices." As such, "one message comes through loud and clear: contrary to the widely shared view of modernity as the first universal civilization, this is a civilization singularly unfit for universalization" (Bauman 1993:215).

By figuratively describing the risk culture of late modern (or postmodern) society as a parasitic organism, we are not saying that Christians should opt for fascism or some other form of explicitly brutal tyranny. Indeed, we must acknowledge that at its best the liberal state and its commercial republic pursue legitimate goods through their institutional artifacts — for example, through the language of rights, exemplified in the United States by the civil rights movement of the 1950s and 1960s — and that they do so in ways that are in certain respects far superior to the other social forms that human beings have devised since the days of Babel.[86] To acknowledge this should not mislead us into believing, however, that liberal society is anything other than a wholly owned subsidiary of a fallen creation. The church cannot, and indeed should not, try to escape to some imaginary realm of pure light free from the taint of sin, but it also should not talk about the space of the secular world as anything other than an extension of a form of life that, in the words of Augustine, reaches back to Babylon, the *civitas terrena* (Augustine, *City of God* 16.4). The Christian community should also always remember that as the *altera civitas* it is on pilgrimage toward a very different realm, that its allegiance and mode of practice is vested in this other city, and that in this world those who love as God loves will frequently, and perhaps invariably, meet with a fate similar to that which met the divine love incarnate.

In light of this fact, we must finally return to where we began, with the question of the church's *modus vivendi* in and with a post-Christendom era. What does the church have to offer to such a time as this? Must Christians resign themselves, as many within and without the body of Christ argue, to our postmodern fate, trying with others to make this particular social order work, thus perpetuating (albeit in greatly truncated and secularized form) the pattern of sponsorship that characterized the ancient regime of Christendom? But if we refuse this path, as I have advocated throughout this book, how can we intelligibly and coherently speak of the mission of the church as an outpost of heaven at this point in history and in this place? It is to these questions that we will now turn.

5

Madness, Truth, and Diaspora:
The Post-Christendom Form of the Church as *Altera Civitas*

People need not believe in the emptiness and melancholia of the postmodern age or approve of what has happened to their traditional ways of life within a risk culture. It is enough, says Václav Havel, that they behave as though they did, or at least tolerate this culture in silence and learn to get along with those who work with them in this setting. Such practical resignation, however, comes at a very high cost, for they must thereafter *"live within a lie.* They need not accept the lie. It is enough for them to have accepted life with it and in it. For by this very fact, individuals confirm the system, fulfil the system, make the system, *are* the system." The greatest threat to the system, therefore, comes from those who dare to suggest in deed as well as word that there might be an alternative to what Giddens calls the reflexive project of the individual, for as Havel states, living within the lie "can constitute the system only if it is universal. The principle must embrace and permeate everything. There are no terms whatsoever on which it can coexist with living within the truth, and therefore everyone who steps out of line *denies it in principle and threatens it in its entirety*" (Havel 1987:45, 56).

All that the postmodern age finally demands is that people conduct themselves as though its practices and institutions were the only game in town. This is just the way things are, people are repeatedly told, and if they want to accomplish anything they will have to do it on these terms. All those who attempt to think and act otherwise are, in a word, mad. They are mad, says Richard Rorty, not because they subscribe to a mistaken view of the world, but simply because

> there is no way to see them as fellow-citizens of our constitutional democracy, people whose life-plans might, given ingenuity and good will, be fitted in with those of other citizens. They are not crazy because they have mistaken the ahistorical nature of human beings. They are crazy because the limits of sanity are set by what we can take seriously. This, in turn, is determined by our upbringing, our historical situation (Rorty 1988:266–67).[87]

The need to label those who threaten to rock the boat as insane is perfectly understandable, for "as long as appearance is not confronted with reality, it does not seem to be appearance. As long as living a lie is not confronted with living the truth, the perspective needed to expose its mendacity is lacking." But should a group of people appear on the scene who are willing to risk the accusation of madness to offer an alternative way of living and being in the world, "it threatens the very existence of appearance and living a lie in terms of what they are, both their essence and their all-inclusiveness." When the basis of the system

is living a lie, Havel contends, "then it is not surprising that
the fundamental threat to it is living the truth." It does not
matter how large a space this alternative occupies, because
its power does not rely upon its physical attributes but on
its potential to bring to everyone's attention the suspect nature of the system's claims both to reality and to universality
(Havel 1987:56f).

It would only perpetuate the Enlightenment myth of
"the universal man" to suppose that the alternative to living the lie begins or ends with the inner life of individuals,
regardless of whether we concern ourselves with what constitutes the requisite affections, attitudes, or beliefs. The
possibility of life within the truth, with its "existential
dimension (returning humanity to its inherent nature),"
its "noetic dimension (revealing reality as it is)," and its
"moral dimension (setting an example for others)" (Havel
1987:56f), requires the social practices of a certain type of
community, or as Havel refers to it, a parallel *polis*. According to the New Testament, God assembles persons from
every tribe and nation, tongue and people to be just such
a community, so that it can display a holy madness in and
for the sake of the world by living in the truth. "The *logic*
of Christianity," writes John Milbank, "involves the claim
that the 'interruption' of history by Christ and his bride, the
Church, is the most fundamental of events, interpreting all
other events. And it is *most especially* a social event, able to
interpret other social formations, because it compares them
with its own social practice" (Milbank 1990:388).

The invitation of Jesus to a holy madness, to a life of
truthfulness in a parallel *polis* (which in this age *is* salvation) is not a call for Christians to withdraw from the
world. Indeed, those who accept this invitation have neither the means nor the mandate to withdraw from society

and maintain themselves at a distance. On the contrary, as citizens of another city they constitute a subversive presence within "enemy territory." Those who classify the way of the *altera civitas* as an effort to withdraw from the world only offer a counsel of despair, for they are in fact asserting that we have no choice but to resign ourselves to a postmodern fate. Indeed, the centuries-long attempt to provide the world with its spiritual form actually stripped Christians of the practices, institutions, and virtues that would allow them to be of genuine service to postmodern society. In short, not only for its own sake, but for the world's sake, the church need not, indeed must not see itself on a continuum between sectarian withdrawal and secular servitude. It is rather summoned by its Lord to live as a parallel *polis* in the truth, that is, in the sacramental interval between Passion, Pentecost, and Parousia.

Within this interval human beings learn to take on God's triune way of being, which "is not a moral attainment... [but] a way of *relationship* with the world, with other people and with God, an event of *communion*" (Zizioulas 1993:15). If the church is to conduct itself on these terms, it must reacquaint itself with the basics of what is required to live in the truth. As we have noted previously, there are innumerable ways in which the present period is more like the time of the first century than the age of Christendom. And yet for the most part, Christianity remains as Gentile and as wedded to the style of the ancient regime as it ever has been. In this final chapter we will briefly consider the story of Israel as the diasporic people of God. More concretely, we will ask how this social form may serve, as George Lindbeck puts it, as a template to help foster and sustain viable Christian communities in this post-Christian, postmodern world (Lindbeck 1988:190). In this narrative template, we may yet discover the necessary and sufficient conditions for living in the truth, conditions that are not finally conceptual but performative.

Memoria Christi

"How different might have been the story of the last two thousand years on this planet grown old from suffering," writes Howard Thurman, "if the link between Jesus and Israel had never been severed! What might have happened if Jesus, so perfect a flower from the brooding spirit of God in the soul of Israel, had been permitted to remain where his roots would have been fed by the distilled elements accumulated from Israel's wrestling with God!" (Thurman 1949:16). Although Thurman's questions may seem abstract and speculative, they in fact provide a concrete point of departure in our quest for an appropriate ecclesiology and *modus vivendi* with the postmodern risk culture. We need only to redirect the focus of his questions from past to future. What would happen to the church, the body of Christ in the world, if in a post-Christian era it once again drew sustenance from the soil that nourished the incarnate utterance of God?

Time and again in the Torah, the Prophets, the Psalter, and all the other Jewish writings that flow like a mighty river from them, "the claim is made that the creator of the entire universe has chosen to live uniquely on a small ridge called Mount Zion, near the eastern edge of the Judaean hill-country." From the point of view of Assyria, Egypt, Babylon, Persia, Greece, Syria, and Rome, the sheer absurdity of this claim was staggering, and yet the Jews held on to this conviction in spite of the mockery of other nations.[88] And yet, says N. T. Wright, this "is what Jewish monotheism looks like on the ground.... To the extent that Israel thought of her god in 'universal' terms, this universal was from the beginning made known in and through the particular, the material, the historical" (Wright 1992b:247f). The church must reacquaint itself with these basic conditions of truthfulness if it is to recover the ground of history that lay beneath the feet of the Jew, Jesus of Nazareth.[89]

According to these conditions as they are set forth in the biblical narrative and the traditions of both Judaism and Christianity, the truth can never be distilled down into an abstract system of thought or elegant set of propositions. Just as living within a lie depends on the institutions and activities of the modern age for its plausibility and coherence, the alternative also relies on the concrete specifications of a comprehensive way of life that can be sustained only by a commonwealth of a rather distinctive sort. A people must live in the truth, be formed and transformed by the truth, before its members can tell (discern and speak) the truth. The ability to recognize the truth and bear witness to it in deed as well as word requires that persons first be initiated into a social practice that marks out the performative dimensions of life in the truth.

If we follow the overarching contours of the biblical story, inhabiting the truth not only originates within but is still dependent upon the covenant relationship between God and Israel, "for salvation is from the Jews" (John 4:22; cf. Rom. 11:17ff). The particularity and concreteness of living in the truth cannot sever itself for long from the Jewish people, the heirs of the promise to Abraham and Sarah. From their standpoint, the truth is never disembodied, nor is it valid for all except, as Michael Wyschogrod says, "in the most indirect and complicated sense." The grasp of the truth that arises from this covenant "is never a truth beyond history, subsisting in any kind of Platonic heaven. Neither is it a universal morality, as so many modern Jews have thought. . . . Judaism is nothing without the Jewish people. Only this people can bring this truth off, almost like a joke that a particular performer can bring to life but when told by others falls flat" (Wyschogrod 1983:28).

Unlike the reflexivity of the modern and postmodern worlds, the forms of reasoning that take place in this tradition do not place the universal, the eternal, the self, and the transcendent over against the particular, the historical, the corporate, and the immanent in a contrastive relationship.[90] Knowledge of the universal, the eternal, the self, and the transcendent instead arises out of and remains in constant connection with our everyday dealings with the concrete particularities of our own time and place. "God's 'beyond,'" writes Dietrich Bonhoeffer, "is not the beyond of our cognitive faculties. The transcendence of epistemological theory has nothing to do with the transcendence of God. God is beyond in the midst of our life. The church stands, not at the boundaries where human powers give out, but in the middle of the village" (Bonhoeffer 1971:282). The universal intent in the church's affirmations and assertions, an intent that is inseparable from its eschatological orientation, thus presupposes the truthfulness of particular ecclesial practices such as baptism and the Lord's Table.

The understanding of the truth that arises from Israel's covenant with the God whom Christians claim raised Jesus from the dead is therefore partial, or as Paul puts it, as though "seen in a mirror, dimly" (1 Cor. 13:12). As Wyschogrod observes, the story of Israel is "replete with great peaks and deep disappointments." The redemption first promised to Abraham remains therefore in abeyance:

"The Exodus, Sinai, the Temple are all peaks and previews of what is in store for Israel and humanity in the fulfillment. But that fulfillment has not yet occurred, and we are therefore dealing with an uncompleted tale whose outcome we know because of our trust in the source of the promise. Nevertheless, however great our trust, we must not confuse promise with fulfillment" (Wyschogrod 1983:69). Although Christians disagree with Jews over the question of whether the messianic age has already drawn near in the life and ministry of Jesus and his followers, both groups await the coming (and therefore for Christians the final consummation) of the eschatological kingdom.[91]

By contrast, the social regime of Christendom celebrated what Douglas John Hall calls the "triumph of finality." According to this thoroughly realized form of eschatology, the result of several re-narrations of the story of redemption so that it conveniently converges with the dominant social practices and institutions of this age, "the divine work is truly finished already and remains only to be displayed to full view and acknowledged universally" (Hall 1993:99). Wyschogrod also notes this disparity between Judaism and what we have termed Constantinianism: "Christianity sees before it a completed salvation history. Creation to resurrection constitutes a totality of promise and fulfillment that is available to viewing and therefore to thought" (Wyschogrod 1983:69). Over the centuries the content of this viewpoint has changed but its basic tendencies have not. Hall correctly states that the many revisions of conventional theism by modern theologians represent "a strategic updating of Theological triumphalism," and thus are little more than a variation on a very old theme, a desperate attempt "to reinstate a waning emphasis upon the transcendent power of God" (Hall 1993:105f).

In short, those who strive for the truth must understand that they are characters in a story that is moving toward (but has yet to reach) its denouement. As a consequence, although Christians long for the truth, they must also recognize that

> the fullness of truth belongs to God rather than to human language about God. Any theology claiming to speak *the truth* is speaking a word that God alone can speak. For human beings, the knowledge of truth is an eschatological reality.... Meanwhile, in this "time between the times," Christian theology can only speak about what seems to be true. Following the *via negativa,* theology gains its greatest insights when it leaves matters of truth to God and strives, rather, toward verisimilitude — toward what appears to be true. And this is no discredit to theology, for verisimilitude is all we can expect to achieve; the truth subsists in God alone (Cunningham 1991:4).

As the community that sees itself continuing Israel's story "in a new key,"[92] the church only fools itself if it believes that the gospel allows it to comprehend in a grand speculative conceit the whole drama of creation in its full scope and detail. It draws near to the truth, on the other hand, when it eschews the illusion of finality in this age and concerns itself with the relationship between what lasts and what comes last (McClendon 1994:75), for it is here that the particular and the universal, the historical and the eternal, the self and the community, and the immanent and the transcendent converge in patterns of activity that are sacramental, that is to say, mysterious signs of communion with God and unity among all human beings (see Flannery 1992:350).

This way of construing such matters is often referred to as a middle-distance approach to theology. Nicholas Lash states that the strategy of focusing on the middle distance is one

> of hopefulness, of the refusal to succumb either to optimism or despair. Despair is "near-sighted," it allows the sharp and painful edges of existing fact to obliterate from view the possibilities inherent in the present situation. Optimism, on the other hand, is "far-sighted:" its vision wanders to distant horizons which appear attractive because they are, in fact, invisible. To seek to focus both memory and hope on the "middle distance" is to acknowledge that historical understanding, whether religious or secular, is at once possible, provisional and unstable (Lash 1986:65).[93]

The standpoint of the middle distance is possible only within a tradition of inquiry that roots human transcendence, not in the Enlightenment illusion of the universal man, but in the historical indices of narrative memory. As we have already noted, memory testifies to the fact that "the present situation has a context; it . . . is part of a continuity, it is 'made' and so it is not immutable." When we come to know that situations have wider contexts, says Rowan Williams, we achieve a measure of freedom or detachment from (or transcendence of) the limits of the present. We learn that things have not always been as they are now, and thus change can and does occur (Williams 1984:30). The middle distance that characterizes the type of transcendence cultivated by Christian social practice may be aptly described *as memoria passionis, mortis et resurrectionis Jesus Christi* (Metz 1980:197).

As the reference to social practice indicates, the *memoria*

Christi cannot be rightly understood apart from its historical connections with God's chosen people. Although the
image of the kingship of God that informs the narrative
memory of Israel does not by itself specifically *denote* a
particular political commonwealth, it does *connote* the political formation of a people through whom the world is
confronted by God's claim upon it. As a company of pilgrims taking part in what has essentially been "a venture
into the future," this people struggled for centuries to develop a social order that was adequate for the long journey.
Initially they existed as a loose-knit confederation of tribes
that struggled desperately to hold on to a foothold they had
established in the rugged hill country of Canaan. Following
the relative anarchy of this period, there ensued a centuries-
long experiment with the institutions of the monarchy,
culminating in the traumatic experience of the Exile. The
conclusion of this question in the life of this people, "and
the basis on which the fulfillment that came in Jesus moves
on, was not the national identity, which the Maccabees res-
urrect once and which the various zealot movements before
and after the time of Jesus attempted again and again un-
successfully. It was rather the community in the dispersion"
(Yoder 1989:81f).

In recent years many Christian theologians have pointed
to the exile and dispersion of the Jewish people as a model
for the church following the demise of Christendom (see,
for example, Clapp 1996a:146–49; Hall 1989:207, 213,
and 1993:408, 491, 537; Lindbeck 1971:226–43; Rahner
1974:57, 207, 214, and 1991:116–18; and Shenk 1995:83,
100f). We must be careful, however, to avoid the trap of
speculating about an ecclesial ideal. A polity that is unable
to acknowledge and deal seriously with the often whimsical
nature of everyday existence, and especially with its tragic

aspects, is worse than useless. Our focus needs to be with the actual genesis of the church from its roots in historic Judaism *and* its subsequent history. Only to the extent that all theology, and ecclesiology in particular, is the explication of this historical practice, however fragmentary and imperfect we may retrospectively judge that practice to have been up until now, will Christians be able to define for themselves a viable and distinctive *modus vivendi* for a postmodern, post-Christian world.

It lies far beyond the scope of this book to explore the many facets of the Jewish diaspora and its formative role in both postbiblical Jewish history and early Christianity. We can, however, say something about the theological significance of this flexible yet distinct polity that enabled Israel to survive and flourish as a people when every other nation and empire of the ancient world faded from the pages of history. The diasporic polity of postexilic Judaism was not an *ad hoc* strategy to which the people of Israel, solely out of political necessity, resigned themselves during times when their access to secular political power was severely limited. In the thinking of prophets such as Jeremiah, the diasporic community was rather "the path of obedience, a safeguard of identity, protection against the 'lying dreams' of those who would trouble the exiles with unreal promises of restored national pride" (Yoder 1989:82). It proved to be a concrete yet flexible form of communal existence that made sense of exile and dispersion, a mobile culture or society that was viable apart from the means of political self-determination and territorial sovereignty.

The ambiguous situation of diasporic Jews in the Hellenistic world and then in the Roman Empire led to changed conceptions about their own identity and the nature of the Torah. What did it mean to be Israel when this term no longer referred to a political entity in the land of Judaea or Samaria? In this context the Torah came more and more to be seen as a code of laws, "and indeed as a civic constitution, a *politeia*. Israel was a unique people, constituted by its practices and its traditions." For Jews in the Greco-Roman world, says Wayne Meeks, "their organized *politeuma* (or whatever their immigrants' association might be called in a local instance) was...an alternative city. Israel, not Alexandria or Antioch, was their ultimate moral reference point, and Israel was both the local embodiment of Moses' ideal polis and the company of God's people that transcended local boundaries and the boundaries of time" (Meeks 1993:44).

Diasporic Judaism was thus founded, as Daniel Boyarin says, "on common memory of shared space and on the hope for such a shared space in an infinitely deferred future" (Boyarin 1994:245). The historic practices that relate time and space in this distinctive way set the politics of the diasporic community apart from the technical organization of modern states and their commercial republics. Jewish social practice over the centuries has initiated each new generation into a distinctive form of personal and communal identity. Every place they settled, every people with whom they interacted, became a sign of a past that was not over and done with, and of a future that remained to be realized. The Passover seder exemplifies this reconfiguring of time and space, stated with clarity in their affirmation at the outset of the feast ("*We* were Pharaoh's slaves in Egypt, and the LORD our God brought *us* forth from there with a mighty hand and an outstretched arm") and in their concluding acclamation ("Next year in Jerusalem!"). The dispersed people of Israel thus continue to re-member history "as the dialectic of an asking divinity and an answer-refusing, but nevertheless an answer-attempting humanity, the dialogue whose demand is an *eschaton*" (Buber 1967:65).

Orientation in time, rather than control over space, thus characterizes the diasporic *politeia* of the Jewish people. Their poetizing memory of God's reign determines the meaning of particular events and places by inscribing them within its narrative eschatology, relativizing (though not completely severing) what most think of as the "natural" connection between occupation and control of territory and the identity of a people.[94] Life in the truth, in the performative interval between memory and expectation, thus subsumes space within a *social drama* that provides shape and direction to history. This dramatic process of encryption effectively precludes any claim to finality on the part of territorial sovereignty. The very name of Judaism derives from a place where relatively few Jews have resided for any length of time, and then usually under the social and political control of foreign nations. In contrast to the identity of other peoples and nations, therefore, the covenant community of Israel in dispersion constitutes a "city" without walls, a community recognized by its endurance through time rather than extension in space (Milbank 1990:403).[95]

The diasporic polity and politics of first-century Judaism provided the basis on which the surprising plot developments of Israel's story in the life, death, and resurrection of Jesus of Nazareth took historical form.[96] Although the church's proclamation of this man as the Jewish messiah modified, and in some ways transformed, Israel's historic expectations concerning the eschatological reign of God, it did not substantially alter either the essentially incomplete nature of this story or the political form of the community that enacts it. The church, which according to the apostle Paul belongs to "the Israel of God" (Gal. 6:16), is likewise measured by its endurance through time rather than extension in space. As fellow travelers with the people of Israel, the church also conducts its business in the interval between memory and hope, and therefore between what lasts and what comes last. Its eucharistic celebration encodes every time and place between Passion (and by implication, Pentecost), on the one hand, and on the other, *Parousia:*

> For I received from the Lord what I also handed on to you, that the Lord Jesus on the night when he was betrayed took a loaf of bread, and when he had given thanks, he broke it and said, "This is my body that is for you. Do this in remembrance of me." In the same way he took the cup also, after supper, saying, "This cup is the new covenant in my blood. Do this, as often as you drink it, in remembrance of me." For as often as you eat this bread and drink the cup, you proclaim the Lord's death until he comes (1 Cor. 11:23–26).[97]

As this passage indicates, the church's distinctive orientation in time (now as then) is liturgically orchestrated by the *eucharistic re-membering* of the body politic of Christ between Jesus' death and the time of his coming. When we remember Jesus in the Eucharist, says Harmon Smith, "we do not recall him to our minds through an act of memory; in remembering Jesus we do not recall him through our own effort and determination." In and through its act of thanksgiving (which is the meaning of "eucharist"), "the church makes an offering; it offers its thanks, its communal sacrifice, its giving itself away, its losing control in order to be faithful and obedient to the God 'who so loved the world that he gave his only begotten Son' to the end that all who believe in him should not perish but have everlasting life." This is how Christians are re-membered to God, and to one another, "this is how the church becomes the body of Christ" (Smith 1995:64f). The church's poetizing memory, the *memoria Christi,* is continually reenacted in the body politics of the crucified and risen Lord. The pattern of relationships that characterizes life together in the community of Jesus and his friends is principally a eucharistic achievement (Lehmann 1963:65).

Mission, Liturgy, and Diaspora

As a diasporic people re-membered again and again as it makes its way toward "the city that is come" (Heb. 13:14), the church does not merely mark the passage of time. Its citizens are instead "concretely drawn into a share in the vulnerability of God, into a new kind of life and a new identity. They do not receive an additional item called faith; their ordinary existence is not reorganized, found wanting in specific respects and supplemented: it is transfigured as a whole" (Williams 1989:108). Because the whole of their life together is claimed and transfigured by the drawing near of the reign of God, the followers of Christ (like their Jewish brothers and sisters) must constantly attend to those matters that "constitute the corporeality of the people: its flesh, sexuality, commerce, and all those concerns that motivate the majority of any people" (Wyschogrod 1983:24).[98] The relationships fostered within the ecclesial household are not restricted to what modern thought labeled the "private" sphere, but have to do with the activities that make up the business of everyday life: building houses, tending gardens, buying and selling, marrying and giving in marriage, and raising children.

The mission of the church in dispersion is therefore not simply to survive in a sometimes hostile world (though it must survive before it can do anything else).[99] Rather it takes its cue from Jeremiah's admonition to the Jewish exiles in Babylon "to seek the welfare of that city" to which God had sent them (Jer. 29:7). Seeking the peace of the postmodern city need not come at the cost of assimilation (though this will be a constant struggle, as it has always been for a diasporic people), nor does it require that the biblical story be rewritten as the convergence of monotheism and the reflexive project of the individual. The church's mandate as an outpost of heaven in this or any other age is finally not something other than its eucharistic worship. In other words, its primary task is to glorify God in the world, which takes the form, as the Orthodox tradition puts it, of the "liturgy after the liturgy."[100] As a city spread throughout the whole world, "the Israel of God" has a distinctive and invaluable role to play in the contemporary context, one that does not simply perpetuate the mechanisms of a risk culture and its reflexive project of self-identity.

Ironically, the social significance of the liturgy after the liturgy is best seen, not in Byzantine Caesaropapism or the Gelasian doctrine of the two swords, but in the example that the postexilic Jewish community has traditionally sought to provide to the world, an example aimed not at individuals but at other nations. According to Gordon Lafer, the practices and institutions that define Jewish solidarity, the level of obligation that binds them together (and which are distinguished from more minimal obligations Jews have to outsiders), were not designed to be used as a universal template to govern relations among all people regardless of their social commitments. Such (mis)applications of Israel's social practice have been attempted with the best of intentions, says Lafer, usually in the name of fostering a universal brotherhood. But what actually comes out in the

wash has instead been a "universal otherhood." The partic-
ulars of Jewish practice are meant "to be reiterated within
each particular nation. This, then, is the universalist mission
of Judaism: not to be 'a light unto all individuals,' not to establish an international system of justice, but rather to teach
specific nations how to live *as* a nation" (Lafer 1993:196).

   This understanding of Israel's mission to the nations also
informs the kinds of relationships Jews have generally cultivated over the centuries with social institutions outside their
own *polis*. A distinctive style of participation (and of resistance) recurs so many times in the Old Testament and other
Jewish writings of the biblical era that we must surely conceive of it as a kind of social paradigm (Yoder 1989:82).
The examples of Joseph and Daniel, Mordecai and Esther,
Judith and Jonah fill the pages of Scripture, providing a
concrete pattern of engagement that Clapp terms sanctified
subversion. The aim of this rather peculiar *modus vivendi* is
to survive in a world held captive by habits and systems of
mutual self-destruction, and whenever possible "to subvert
it to its own good" (Clapp 1996a:200). As fellow travelers with Israel through the present age, those who make
up the body of Christ must likewise enter fully into the
everyday. The nature of their involvement, also like that of
their Jewish forebears, must be in keeping with the distinctive mission of the church. In short, they are to be "wise as
serpents and innocent as doves" (Matt. 10:16). As a diasporic people Christians must enter into the everyday armed
with carefully cultivated skills of discernment that will allow
them to name the world as created, fallen, and redeemed.

   The critical question of personal identity in our day and
time is in many ways analogous to the situation described in
the Book of Daniel. Although for most of us the crisis of
identity does not involve persecution as it did for Daniel

and his friends, "but seduction into false notions of the self," there are nonetheless important similarities. "In both situations," says Walter Brueggemann, "the invitation to an alternative sense of self depends on an alternative articulation, by the storyteller, by the poet, by the preacher. The Daniel stories, then, model an alternative personal identity that was crucial in that ancient persecution and is crucial in our contemporary seduction" (Brueggemann 1989:114). We must take Brueggemann's analysis one step further. Stories that articulate an alternative identity do not stand alone, but are set within social practices that place this identity beyond the reach of either the persecutor or the seducer. Baptism, table fellowship, disciplines of forgiveness and reconciliation, prayer and fasting, and habits of hospitality that nurture friendships with the poor and outcast enable the followers of Jesus to withstand the pressure of both overt persecution and the subtle seduction of the postmodern risk culture.

Self-identity within the body politic of Christ thus has little to do with the Enlightenment's working hypothesis of the universal man or the contrivances of individual reflexive projects. It is vested instead in a dramatic process, flowing from the poetic contours of memory, that is both fluid and elusive. This process bequeaths to each character in the drama a wide range of possible responses, and each response in turn makes sense only in terms of a story that is constantly unfolding. The self thus truly is, as Rowan Williams puts it, "what the past is doing now, it is the process in which a particular set of 'given' events and processes and options crystallizes now in a new set of particular options, responses and determinations, providing a resource of given pastness out of which the next decision and action can flow" (Williams 1984:30, 29). As with any dramatic sequence, there are certain constraints on how the performance of this tale can continue, and "within those constraints there are indefinitely many ways that it can continue" (MacIntyre 1984:201).

The identities of those within the *altera civitas* thus take shape over time as characters in a narrative history that begins and ends in the life of the triune God. This narrative generates a vast array of options, responses, and determinations that allow for innovative ways of dealing with the world. For example, we see in the so-called otherworldliness of the African American spiritual how self-identity formed within the eschatological framework of the biblical story engages with the authorities and powers of this age. Gayraud Wilmore contends that this otherworldliness is in fact a complex phenomenon that connects without confusing the hope of heaven in the hereafter and the hope of liberation in the here and now. In these congregations, says Wilmore, "the hope for the Kingdom to come provides the motivating power for living. . . . Eschatology, in other words, dominates and regulates the self-understanding and behavior of an eschatological people" (Wilmore 1982:67). James McClendon rightly concludes that the spiritual "is at once a celebration of the hereafter and a present claim upon the here and now — if heaven is not Apartheid country, singers will be free to shout all over it; should they not therefore be free all over earth as well?" (McClendon 1994:90).[101]

The way that African American spirituals connect social setting and personal identity within an eschatological vector reiterates the practice of both diasporic Judaism and early Christianity. The significance of these connections comes clearly into view when contrasted with the reflexive project of self-identity that we examined in the previous chapter. The technical organization that underwrites this project promotes a specific form of knowledge, "one sustained and determined by the power to provide oneself with one's own place. . . . In other words, *a certain power is the precondition of this knowledge* and not merely its effect or its attribute. It makes this knowledge possible and at the same time determines its characteristics. It produces itself in and through this knowledge" (de Certeau 1984:36). The knowledge environments produced by this technical regime treat time and space as a field of operations that is subject to a strategic calculus of power relationships. This type of knowledge *qua* power subsists within the wide variety of agonistic relationships generated by modern social institutions between individuals and groups (as each tries to secure her, his, or its own possessions, interests, and selfhood from others). As this power/knowledge circulates through these relationships it not only consolidates its hold on everything that falls within its reach, but it also seeks to expand its territory.

Within this technical reconfiguration of the world, the self-positing or reflexive subject becomes the sole locus of all choice and action. This peculiarly modern subject need not be an individual human being, but any number of entities endowed with will and power; for example, a business, an army, a state, or a scientific institution. According to Michel de Certeau, the subject "seeks first of all to distinguish its 'own' place, that is, the place of its own power and will, from an 'environment.'" The subject thus "postulates a *place* that can be delimited as its *own* and serve as the base from which relations with an *exteriority* composed of targets or threats . . . can be managed." The Cartesian attitude that characterizes modern science, the politics of the nation-state, and military strategy is clearly recognizable in the "effort to delimit one's own place in a world bewitched by the invisible powers of the Other" (de Certeau 1984:xix, 35–37).

Among the objectives sought by the self-positing subject is the triumph of its own place over time, or as Anthony Giddens puts it, the colonization of the future. The traditional conception of history as a continuing story for which humans are neither the sole nor the final authors, and thus as an inheritance that "requires of those who receive it that they shall both develop it in the present and hand it on to the future," has no place in a postmodern risk culture. In such a culture there is "no future and there is no past. There is only the moment which has been rescued from the void, and the desire to snatch from the void the next moment as well" (Bonhoeffer 1955:105). By designating its place as separate from all others, the reflexive subject seeks at every moment to capitalize on acquired advantages, prepare for future expansions, and secure an optimal degree of independence over against the variability of circumstance. The claims of practices and institutions inherited from the past are quickly dismissed as allochronic, "belonging to a different time, and surviving into the present on false pretenses ... merely relics doomed to extinction" (Bauman 1993:39).

The postmodern subject also strives from its privileged position to master other spaces. This objective is accomplished through strategies that are designed to "transform foreign forces into objects that can be observed and measured, and thus control and 'include' them within its scope of vision. To be able to see (far into the distance) is also to be able to predict, to run ahead of time by reading a space" (de Certeau 1984:36). The significance of other people, places, and things — once determined by local activities and relationships in such a way that "persons were not

'individuals' at all but overlapping members one of another"
(Clapp 1996a:91) — is re-encoded within technical environments of power/knowledge that pivot around the place
of the subject. The privileged place of the reflexive subject
serves "as the basis for generating relations with an exterior
distinct from it (competitors, adversaries, 'clientèles,' 'targets,' or 'objects' of research)."[102] With respect to both time
and space, the triumph of finality once claimed by Constantinian society has now been usurped by the technical
mechanisms of the post-Cartesian risk culture.

In contrast, the *modus vivendi* of the diasporic community is specifically determined by the lack of its own place.
It is unable (and hopefully unwilling) to designate a proper
locus from which to contain and manage those who sur-
round it. Its place is therefore the space of the *other,* and
its social form is that of the parallel *polis.* The members of
such a community do not have the wherewithal to plan a
general strategy or to view the adversary as a whole within
a distinct space, but see themselves living and acting upon a
terrain they did not choose, a terrain organized by a foreign
power. In the words of de Certeau, this kind of community
"does not have the means to keep to itself, at a distance,
in a position of withdrawal, foresight, and self-collection:
it is a maneuver 'within the enemy's field of vision,' as
von Bülow put it, and within enemy territory" (de Certeau
1984:37).[103] A people in dispersion knows that it does not
control the processes through which the goods of society
are identified, produced, or distributed, but must learn to
deal creatively and redemptively with the persons, practices,
and institutions that do control these means.

In place of strategy as the defining disposition of modern
science, economics, and military planning, the community
in dispersion must practice the "art of the weak." A people

well versed in this art operates in discrete actions, without setting aside a designated place where it can stockpile its winnings for the next encounter. This "nowhere" provides a type of tactical mobility, but it forgoes the pretense of stability and control, relying instead on the ability to take advantage of the opportunities that present themselves only at particular times and places. Its *modus vivendi* within a modern risk culture is therefore to concentrate on "everyday practices that produce without capitalizing, that is, without taking control over time" (de Certeau 1984:xx, 37). Because it gives up all claims to both space and time, a diasporic people must therefore rely ultimately on the providential activity of God for its survival and prosperity.

For the Jewish people, diaspora has meant that for over three millennia they have deliberately cultivated the social role of the *other* in the world, even in their ancestral land (Boyarin 1994:243). They learned to survive, and whenever possible to flourish, on terrain organized by those who did not recognize God's sovereign claim on the whole of creaturely existence. They developed, refined, and passed on to succeeding generations practices and skills that enabled them to exist — for the time being, and in whatever place they found themselves — as the other. The *modus vivendi* of this community has been vested in everyday practices that produce without capitalizing, without taking control over time. It is not an easy existence to maintain, and the temptations to "capitalize" are omnipresent, for example, in the experiments in statecraft undertaken not only in the modern nation-state of Israel, but also in the United States.[104] But a diaspora existence is the way the people of God have for most of their history nurtured life in the truth.

The politics of diaspora allowed the identity and creativity of the Jewish people to continue and prosper while

at the same time making it possible for them to participate fully (though judiciously) in the common life of their
surroundings. From this combination of distinctive identity and discerning engagement they learned that "cultures
are not preserved by protecting from 'mixing' but probably
can only continue to exist as a product of such mixing. All
cultures, and identities, are constantly being remade." Judaism's diasporic politics laid this process bare because it
could not define itself as a self-enclosed, bounded phenomenon, but instead sustained a distinct identity as a people
over the centuries apart from the "natural" association of
nationhood and land. The distinguishing mark of Judaism's
diasporic identity, in short, lay in its disaggregated character
(Boyarin 1994:243). When measured by endurance through
time rather than extension in and control over space, the
disaggregated commonwealth of postbiblical Judaism has
been its unrecognized strength.

According to the New Testament, the body politic of
Christ should also be known by the absence of control
as measured from the strategic perspective of a "proper
place" and its "postulation of power" (de Certeau 1984:38).
When regarded from this tactical standpoint, the confrontation between God's messianic regime and those rulers
and authorities who currently exercise their dominion over
the world no longer seems like the husk of a primitive
apocalyptic mythology that can be stripped away without
damaging the kernel of true religion within. Under the
tutelage of such myths[105] diasporic politics prepares the pilgrim people of God to be the bearer of habits and relations
that locates all of life within the context of a promised but
as yet unfulfilled future, thereby defying the darkness of
the secular void. The ecclesial practices that sustain these
pilgrims give distinctive shape and direction, sense and co-

herence, to their use of those goods that comprise everyday life. By deliberately cultivating the distinctive identity as the *other* city in the postmodern world, the church through its own weakness exhibits the power of God's eschatological rule as a historical possibility and actuality.

Diasporic politics also supplies the basis on which Christians relate to those whom we encounter as the other. The other is not only the brother or sister within the social fellowship of the church, but also those of other races, cultures, and traditions. The other is the colleague with whom we work daily within the technical organization of the postmodern world. The other is the neighbor with whom Christians must live and make sense of a shared existence, and in whose company we stand continually before God. One of the most tragic features of postmodern life is the absence of the grace necessary to allow the other to *be* other, and thus to receive her or his differences as gift, in an act of "self-affirmation that is also a self-displacement, since it seeks to resituate [the] self through the address of others toward me" (Milbank 1995:132). A risk society, on the other hand, effectively effaces difference by assimilating it into its own peculiar notion of what it means to be human: an unencumbered and empty subject set over against other unencumbered and empty selves, each wanting "to be soothed, organized, and made cohesive by...the experience of being continually filled up by consuming goods, calories, experiences, politicians, romantic partners, and empathic therapists in an attempt to combat the growing alienation and fragmentation of its era" (Cushman 1990:600).

The politics of the *altera civitas,* by contrast, strives to give to others a place where they can be who and what they were created to be from the infinite fullness of God's own triune love. To give someone love, says Herbert Mc-Cabe, "is to give her herself, to give him himself, to let him be.... Love is the space in which to expand, and it is always a gift. In this sense we receive ourselves at the hands of others. Of course this is true in innumerable ways — we have to be born of others, for a start — but our growth, our personal development, also takes place only in the space that others provide by their love" (McCabe 1987:108). To love, in other words, is a performative response *in* love and obedience to the gift of being human. In and through this response we give to those we love a concrete place where they can be who and what God created them to be. In place of the universal man posited by Descartes' *cogito, ergo sum,* therefore, the church proposes a radically different starting point for all thought and action: *Deus amat, ergo sumus.*[106] From this ecclesial standpoint we learn that the purpose of our very being is to love as God loves.

The mission of the church is thus to reveal to the world its *arche* and *telos* by offering to it the means and media for living in love and therefore in the truth. The ecclesial habits and relations that ferment a lifestyle of truth in the midst of the present age are indeed sacramental, for they supply the citizens of the diasporic commonwealth with the wherewithal to take advantage of opportunities that this world affords them. The performative grasp of the truth does not therefore reside in the abstractions of a worldview, but preeminently in patterns of human action cultivated by the citizens of a parallel city who, in spite of their incredible diversity, fragility, and fallibility, bear the body of the risen Christ to the world. These sacramental patterns "force to light hidden directions and dispositions that would otherwise never come to view, and thus make the conflicts of goals and interests between people a *public* affair" (Williams

1989:96). Christian social practice in a postmodern context, with its never-ending negotiations with the institutions and expectations of a risk culture, is finally nothing other than a sacramental project for living in the truth.

The postmodern risk culture and the diasporic politics of the church thus constitute alternative social orders that afford very different possibilities for being and becoming human in the world. One claims exclusive rights over the present age. The other nurtures possibilities for living that the former cannot even imagine while awaiting the revelation of a commonwealth in which death, "the shroud that is cast over all peoples, the sheet that is spread over all nations" (Isa. 25:7), will no longer have the final word. Until then the people of God must learn how to go on and go further in a world that "like a woman with child...writhes and cries out in her pangs when she is near her time" (Isa. 25:7; 26:17). The body politic of Christ, if it is to sustain this way of being in and relating to a fallen world, must develop the requisite skills and relations to create and maintain the kind of "holy insecurity" (see Harvey 1994:217–41) that distinguishes it from its neighbors in the postmodern city. The citizens of the *altera civitas* must always struggle to detect the delicate counterpoint of the Spirit that mediates between creative engagement (through which they seek the welfare of the postmodern city) and nonconformity (acknowledging their status as aliens residing for a time within its walls).

There are no pat, once-and-for-all formulas that will draw an unambiguous line between conformity and nonconformity, or relieve a particular congregation of the burden of deciding which institutions and practices of the postmodern city to reject in their entirety, which to accept within limits, and which to simultaneously embrace and redefine within the household of faith. As noted above, the art of the weak relies on the ability to take advantage of those opportunities that present themselves at particular times and places. At certain times in the past, for example, the church found creative and redemptive uses for such institutions as the antique *paterfamilias* and medieval serfdom.[107] In our own day Christians must likewise struggle to make the best use of the structures of a risk culture — in particular, the institutions of wage labor and the market, and the coercive mechanisms of the nation-state — that otherwise enforce an economy of desire ordered around habits of self-absorbed consumption. Baptism, eucharistic fellowship, traditions of interpretation, finely tuned patterns of authority, and the practice of forgiveness and reconciliation empower the body of Christ to improvise new ways to transform time and space into signs of the liberating rule of God.

Finally, this brief consideration of diasporic politics would be incomplete without addressing one more topic. "With no new houses in prospect," says Lash, "we have to learn to live in tents. Christians, like Jews, are (or should be) nomads and, as such, should function as *prophetic* irritants (or, as they say, 'subversives') to the builders of cities" (Lash 1988:216). Because a diasporic polity and politics is at odds with the practices and institutions that organize life in the postmodern city, it always constitutes a potential threat to that society. A people whose political and personal identity is not coterminous with state or ethnic boundaries simply does not fit neatly into the established categories that assign personal identity within a risk culture. We must therefore take note of the cost that the members of Christ's body will invariably incur by practicing this way of life.

Once again the church should look to the narrative history of postbiblical Judaism for insight into the meaning of sanctified subversion. Boyarin notes that "Jewishness disrupts the very categories of identity because it is not national, not genealogical, not religious, but all of these, in dialectical tension with one another" (Boyarin 1994:244). The confusion of categories is more than a little unsettling to the rulers and authorities of our age, because the purpose of these categories is to cleanly (that is, without discussion) distribute such matters along the divide between what is private and what is public. A diasporic people frustrates this design by bringing to the light of day the true nature of the technical organization and reflexive reasoning that govern day-to-day existence within the postmodern city. As such it poses an enormous threat to the powers that be, for the techniques and strategies used by self-positing subjects to construct knowledge environments habitually seek to "conceal beneath objective calculations their connection with power that sustains them from within the stronghold of [their] own 'proper' place or institution" (de Certeau 1984:xx).

Because of its disruptive character, diasporic politics will therefore be considered by many in the postmodern city as subversive. Havel puts it well when he notes that because "the main pillar of the system is living a lie, then it is not surprising that the fundamental threat to it is living the truth. This is why it must be suppressed more severely than anything else" (Havel 1987:56f). According to Wyschogrod, it is precisely in this context "that Jewish sacrifice must be seen. The Jewish people must be and is prepared to be sacrificed for the sanctification of God's name." This is a truth that is dreadful to contemplate, and it is not at all certain that Israel should know it. Wyschogrod hastens to add that this is a truth that must be understood dialectically, for otherwise it could be realized only by a self-loathing people that seeks death, and Israel knows itself to be cherished as no other people has been (the Song of Songs, a love story, is read at the synagogue during the Sabbath of Passover). And yet "it 'knows' that its existence is an invitation to aggression and that by raising Jewish children it is raising the sacrifices of the future and that the dreadful future will come, no matter how long the peaceful intervals may be" (Wyschogrod 1983:24).

The continuing relationship of the Christian community to the story of the Jewish people manifests itself clearly at this point, and so provides a fitting conclusion to our study. As McCabe emphasizes, the gospel of Jesus Christ gives concrete voice to two antithetical truths "which express the tragedy of the human condition: the first is that if you do not love you will not be alive; the second is that if you *do* love you will be killed. If you cannot love you remain self-enclosed and sterile, unable to create a future for yourself or others, unable to live. If, however, you do effectively love you will be a threat to the structures of domination upon which our human society rests and you will be killed" (McCabe 1987:218). The otherness of the *altera civitas* bears witness to the continuing drama of living within the truth, in which the members of Christ's body give their assent by offering their bodies as a living sacrifice to God (Rom. 12:1).

Notes

―――――

Introduction

1. The groove of the City is not limited to the developed nations in Asia, Europe, and North America, but can be seen throughout the world. In postapartheid South Africa, for example, these forces are proving irresistible to the new regime led by the African National Congress. See Beinart 1997:23–26.

2. Even differences of race are governed by the logic of boutique multiculturalism, as Afro-American expression in music and sport becomes "useful cultural capital" servicing the demands of commodification and consumption in America's commercial republic (Jennings 1996).

3. This is the concern, in many ways quite legitimate, of Stern in his fascinating book (1961). And yet in the final analysis the root of despair is not pessimism or cynicism, though these can certainly exacerbate a situation, but a false hope.

4. In addition to the recent work of O'Donovan, perhaps the most influential voice in this regard is that of Newbigin (1986).

5. For two interesting examples of this response to the demise of Christendom, see Markham 1994 and Hodgson 1994.

6. For a superb critique of the modern contraction of politics into statecraft, see Michael Baxter 1994:425–48.

Chapter 1: An Outpost of Heaven

7. For a thorough treatment of the way the Romans regarded the early Christians, see Wilken 1984.

8. Wright adds in this regard that "from a Roman point of view it would be the similarities between Judaism and Christianity that

would stand out. The Christians in Bithynia in 110, and in Smyrna in 155, shared some salient characteristics with the Jews of the pre-70 era. In particular, their worldview looks suspiciously as though it included a Jewish-style adherence to the kingship of god" (Wright 1992b:350).

9. In recent years missiologists and others refer to this convergence of church and mission under the category of the *missio Dei,* the mission of God. See Bosch 1991:390–93.

10. Elshtain (1987) also examines the presumption of original violence.

11. In his typical candor Rorty (1988) reveals himself to be the "natural" heir of Hobbes and the ontology of violence when he argues that one must put liberal politics first and tailor a philosophy to suit.

12. As Wink puts it, the gods never died, "they only became diseases" (1986:116).

Chapter 2: The City That Is to Come

13. "Theological rhetoric," says David Nicholls, "child of political experience, may also be mother of political change" (1989:14).

14. See Lash's insightful essay on the performative meaning of the biblical images (1986:37–61).

15. This, of course, is a sticking point with many in the academy, most notably with those who embrace the viewpoint of the so-called Jesus Seminar, the findings of which are published in Funk, Hoover, et al. 1993. Space does not permit delving into this christological debate. Many excellent critiques have been written in connection with the claims of the seminar. A particularly engaging response is Hays 1994:43–48.

16. Some may be concerned that the idea of poetizing memory excludes or limits the historicity of these accounts in particular and of the divine rule in general. Although space does not permit a detailed response, suffice it so say that the idea of history itself is not a given but is constantly taking shape within the tensions of time and space.

17. The notion that such things as facts (discrete packets of raw experience unrelated to any kind of theory) actually exist was an

invention of the Enlightenment. For a delightful discussion of the emergence of this notion, see Daston 1994:37–63.

18. There are important connections between what Buber terms poetizing memory and the so-called precritical tradition of biblical exegesis practiced by the church (and in a somewhat different form by the synagogue) for over a millennium. Space does not permit detailing these links here, but for further discussion see Freeman 1993:21–28; Frei 1974; and Steinmetz 1980:27–38.

19. As Walter Wink observes, the basic theme of original violence in the *Enuma Elish* is not limited to Mesopotamia but is repeated in similar myths in Syria, Phoenicia, Egypt, Germany, Ireland, and India (Wink 1992:14f).

20. Far from offering an alternative to these myths, Milbank argues, modern secular practice and thought is from the outset "complicit with an 'ontology of violence,' a reading of the world which assumes the priority of force and tells how this force is best managed and confined by counter-force" (1990:4).

21. Buber uses the German term *Unbändigkeit*, which means something like "unfetteredness," or more loosely, "the refusal of all limits."

22. As more than one person has pointed out, in Scripture true freedom is a matter of being the slaves of God.

23. For our purposes the historical question of whether this fundamental impulse in the life of Israel originally derived from the time of the Exodus or the period of the judges is immaterial. See in this regard Albright 1957:254ff; Bright 1953:17–22; and Gottwald 1979.

24. To suppose, as biblical scholar Norman Gottwald does, "that for a certain brief moment, not traceable in the texts, the ancient Israelites arrived at Kantian insights: they distinguished morality from custom, ritual, and religion, and already realized that theological representations, while not 'operationable' like empirical concepts, still had a regulative function, giving a certain 'onlook towards *praxis*,'" is an anachronistic conceit that quickly dissipates into thin air under critical scrutiny (Milbank 1990:113; cf. Gottwald 1979:608–37, 693f, 703f).

25. The enigmatic character of Ecclesiastes, in contrast to a pessimistic interpretation, is emphasized by Ogden 1987.

26. The idea of beginning in Jewish and Christian theology also has two distinct senses. To speak of the world as having been called into being out of nothing is to acknowledge God as the beginning, the *archê* or *principium,* of the world. The term can also refer to the world's inception as time and space.

27. Stanley Hauerwas says in this regard that "apocalyptic does not deny the continuation of the history of creation but rather reminds us it is historical exactly because it has an end" (1988b:51).

28. Wright adds that "it was the Stoics, not the first-century Jews, who characteristically believed that the world would be dissolved in fire" (1992b:285).

29. We will encounter this strategy of dismissing the past as "allochronic," belonging to a bygone era and surviving into the present on false pretenses, again in the fourth and fifth chapters of this volume.

30. For a survey of messianic expectations leading up to the first century C.E., see Wright 1992b:307–20. For an excellent example of how the idea of a messiah has been treated in Jewish circles, see Scholem 1971.

31. Although the New Israel includes Gentiles, who at one time were "aliens from the commonwealth of Israel, and strangers to the covenants of promise" (Eph. 2:12), Messianic Israel (that is, the church in Christ) does not exclude Jews. In other words, although the being and mission of the church are not identical to those of postbiblical Judaism, the overarching witness of the New Testament steadfastly maintains that the body of Christ exists in historical continuity with the being of the Jewish people (and then only by the grace of God). Christian faith, linked to the continuing existence of Israel by the divine economy of creation and redemption articulated in Scripture, is finally nothing other than the particular, material, and historical life in community that the followers of Christ live with and before God, with and before the world. For a masterful analysis of the ongoing relationship of the church to its Jewish origins in the New Testament see Hays 1996:407–43.

32. I am indebted to McClendon 1994:67 for the basic out-

line describing these modifications to Israel's understanding of the kingship of God.

33. It should be emphasized that although the events surrounding the passion of Jesus and the subsequent suffering of his followers do bring the cost of giving allegiance to the God of Israel into sharper focus, this price has long been known to Israel. As we will discuss in more detail in the last chapter, the Jewish people have known for some time that they must be, as Michael Wyschogrod puts it, "prepared to be sacrificed for the sanctification of God's name" (1983:24).

34. Hauerwas makes a similar observation about the history of Abraham's people in the Old Testament. This connection between the children of Abraham according to the flesh and the children of Abraham according to faith certainly puts a new and sobering slant on what it means to share in the faith of Abraham (Rom. 4:16). He also reminds us that "they remained faithful enough so that they might be truthful about their unfaithfulness" (1988b:49).

Chapter 3: Rendering to Caesar the Things That Are God's

35. This does not mean that the beliefs or doctrines are incidental to this common life by any stretch of the imagination. Rather, it means that they are like threads in a garment: once they are removed from that piece of cloth they lose all texture and coherence. Christian doctrine in a post-Christian era must likewise be rooted in and nourished by the soil of ecclesial practices that order the common life of its members, or like its modern counterparts it will wither and die on the vine.

36. Although most scholars would date the split between Christianity and Judaism in either the later first or early second century c.e., some have recently argued that a substantial Jewish presence existed in the church, particularly among those in the diaspora, as late as the early fifth century. See Stark 1996:49-71.

37. The question of whether it is accurate to refer to the changes that took place during this period of time as the Constantinian shift is widely debated. Many in the patristic era celebrated the first "Christian emperor" as a sign of divine providence, pronouncing his reign a pattern of Christ's heavenly kingdom. Eusebius, for example,

compared him favorably to Moses in the dispensation of salvation, leading his people from the captivity of persecution (Eusebius, *The History of the Church* 9.9.5–6, *Life of Constantine* 1.12). In our own century Charles Cochrane called him the "architect (to a very great extent) of the Middle Ages" (1940:211). To such minds his conversion marked the beginning of the "Christian era." More recent scholarship generally takes a different view. Stark, for example, contends that Constantine's conversion was an expedient response to, rather than the cause of, the exponential growth of the church during the latter half of the third century (1996:5, 10). Historian Averil Cameron concurs with Stark, arguing that "Constantine marks a convenient but not an all-important landmark" in the spread of Christianity within the empire (1991:13). Although it is certainly the case that Constantine's "conversion" was neither the sole nor the most important cause of the changes that took place, the unofficial prestige that the church soon enjoyed, and the official recognition that would come a few decades later, would not have come about were it not for his initial toleration of and personal identification with Christianity. Stark and Cameron thus tend to overcompensate for past indiscretions. Constantine represents an important moment in the rapidly changing circumstances of the church with respect to its identity and mission and thus with regard to its relationship to the world about it.

38. So says R. A. Markus in an otherwise splendid interpretation of Augustine's ecclesiology (1970:178ff).

39. These institutions treat the symptoms of a fallen creation, as it were, but should not be considered a "cure."

40. O'Donovan also notes that prior to the time of Constantine Christian apologists identified the rise of the Roman Empire as a sign of the rout of demons, the plurality of nations previous to it being an aspect of polytheism (O'Donovan 1996:198).

41. Cf. Luke 20:25. Yoder rightly observes that "the 'spiritualizer's' picture of a Jesus whose only concern about politics was to clarify that he was not concerned for politics is refuted by the very fact that this question could arise. In the context of his answer 'the things that are God's' most normally would not mean 'spiritual things'; the attribution 'to Caesar Caesar's things and to God God's

things' points rather to demands or prerogatives which somehow overlap or compete, needing to be disentangled. What is Caesar's and what is God's are not on different levels, so as never to clash; they are in the same arena" (Yoder 1994a:44f).

42. Eusebius, *In Praise of Constantine* 6.2.

43. Cf. *The History of the Church* 10, 1.3, 6. The biblical citations are from Ps. 72:7–8 and Isa. 2:4.

44. Cf. 8.24, 11.16, 20.11. For more on the influence of Tyconius on Augustine's later ecclesiology, see Markus 1970:115–122.

45. Other examples of efforts to reestablish the missional *modus vivendi* of the early church as a distinct society or *polis* can be found at many and various times in later church history. O'Donovan lists the papalist revolution of the eleventh century, the mendicant movement of the thirteenth and fourteenth centuries, and the Calvinist and Tridentine reforms of the late sixteenth century as specific attempts to reassert the vis-à-vis of apostolic and patristic Christianity. We should certainly add the development of monasticism after the third century to this list. But as O'Donovan himself is aware, these efforts, which centered on establishing further differentiations within Christian society, unwittingly served to reinforce the division of labor that cast the church as the spiritual form of a secular body politic (1996:196, 207).

46. McClendon notes in this regard that the context of Anselm's thought "was legal — there was the jurisprudential character of Latin theology from Tertullian onward, the lingering imperial law in the former provinces, the canon law expressed in the church's penitential practice and in the governance of his abbey at Bec, the Germanic customary law with its *Wergild* or compensatory payment made to avert retribution by another" (McClendon 1994:205). For intriguing analyses of Anselm's seminal influence on later Western history, see Gorringe 1996 and O'Donovan 1996:205f.

47. For a more detailed description of the differences between Christendom in East and West, see Guroian 1987:119–24.

48. I am deeply indebted on this matter to a splendid essay by William T. Cavanaugh (1995:397–420).

49. This is a practice that continues unabated in the our own time. We only need remember on this score how the American pres-

ident George Bush unilaterally invoked the theological category of just war at the start of the Persian Gulf war. Other examples abound in Northern Ireland, South Africa, and the Middle East, not to mention the shameless way impoverished whites were manipulated to serve the interests of the ruling aristocracy of the American South before and after the Civil War. See Silver 1957 and Smith 1972.

50. The rest of the world did take notice. Even such Roman antagonists as Celsus, Galen, and Julian the Apostate not only conceded that the conduct of Christians was extraordinary, but that it played an important role in the growth of the movement. See Wilken 1984:82.

51. See below for more details about the innovative political character of the modern nation-state.

52. The ambiguity that permeates this state of affairs underlies much of the current disagreement among North American Baptists regarding the relationship of the church to liberal democratic institutions. See in this regard Curtis W. Freeman, "Can Baptist Theology Be Revisioned?" *Perspectives in Religious Studies* 24 (Fall 1997): 273–302.

53. In effect, the church repeated the expressed desire of the early Israelites to become like other nations (1 Sam. 8:4, 20).

54. I am alluding here of course to H. Richard Niebuhr's important book (1970). I do not mean to suggest that Niebuhr is somehow solely responsible for the continuation of Constantinianism, but only that he expresses in splendid fashion precisely how it does indeed continue to the present day.

55. The fact that these axioms coincide perfectly with what Mullins contends are the core Baptist beliefs only confirms for him their rectitude. We see here the same kind of realized eschatology that we encountered in the fourth century, revealing Mullins to be a latter-day Eusebius.

56. The scandal of the evangelical mind, which according to Mark Noll is "that there is not much of an evangelical mind," is rooted in this relocation of Christian piety exclusively in the affections (1994:3).

57. J. C. O'Neill makes an interesting case for viewing monasticism as a part of the church since the days of the apostles,

continuing a practice that had its origins in Judaism. If true, this would constitute yet another important link between early Christianity and its origins in Jewish soil (1989:270–87).

58. For further information on this double ethical standard, with different requirements for the ordinary Christian living in the everyday world and for ascetics striving to realize Christ's maxim to be perfect, see Baynes 1955:24–46 and Brown 1988:204–209. If O'Neill's thesis above is correct, it would go a long way in explaining why both Augustine and John Chrysostom sought over against this development to reintegrate the monastic life with that of ordinary Christians, emphasizing in their writings on monasticism that there is but one final end toward which all must strive, and one moral standard to which all must subscribe. See Guroian 1994:133–54 and Markus 1990:63–83; cf. 1990:157–211.

59. Taylor points out that these traits not only constituted the essence of what Max Weber calls the "innerworldly asceticism" of Puritanism, but it also provided a hospitable environment for the scientific revolution and its instrumental understanding of reason (1989:223; cf. 1989:222, 225, 230–33).

60. An excellent example of this kind of accommodation was recently provided in a statement on "Christian Conscience and Citizenship," signed by forty-two Protestant, Roman Catholic and Orthodox Christians and published in the periodical *First Things*. The sole theological basis for their understanding of Christian citizenship is the passing reference in the American Declaration of Independence to "the law of nature and of nature's God" (Various 1997:51–54).

Chapter 4: Romancing Divinity

61. The generic Hebrew word for human being, '*adam*, is derived from the word '*adamah*, "earth." Insofar as the etymology of Scripture is concerned, then, the human being is not a thinking thing, but an earth thing.

62. As with Constantine, the notion of a "Cartesian shift" does not mean that Descartes single-handedly brought about the changes associated with the Enlightenment. It is rather an acknowledgment

that the ideas and images in his philosophy served as an important catalyst in what subsequently transpired.

63. This is the premise of foundationalism, for which Descartes deserves much of the credit or blame, depending upon one's viewpoint. Many so-called postmodern authors continue to struggle against this image, and in the process perpetuate its basic ordinations, but in an antithetical mode.

64. This is a debate that David Brown presupposes but does not question in his book on the Trinity (1985). See in this regard Buckley 1987. It is important to note that, according to Nicholas Lash, when the word "theism" first appeared in English in 1678 it was interchangeable with "deism." Both terms originally denoted belief in a Supreme Being as the source of the finite world, joined together with a rejection of revelation and the "supernatural doctrines" of Christianity. For further discussion see Lash 1988:105.

65. Stephen Toulmin tends to idealize the Renaissance conceptions of this strictly human realm over against his harsh critique of the Enlightenment in his superb work *Cosmopolis* (1990). Although there is some truth to this distinction, to juxtapose the two in this fashion overlooks their essential connections.

66. Some elements of the modern vision predate the Renaissance. For example, according to Milbank, a conception of God as "a radical divine simplicity without real or formal differentiation, in which, most commonly, a proposing 'will' is taken to stand for the substantial identity of will, essence and understanding," originally formulated by medieval nominalism and voluntarist theology, was crucial to the modern portrait of the human being as a self-positing, self-possessing subject (1990:14).

67. David Burrell rightly notes that Aquinas did not intend with the ideas of nature and grace to distinguish between the world of nature as the realm of physical reality whose fixed laws comprise the subject matter of natural science, and the world of history as the realm of freedom whose tendencies are assigned to the "human" sciences (Burrell 1993:3f, 93f). Nevertheless, they served to further separate, ever so slightly, eschatology from ecclesiology, providing a wedge that others used to split creation asunder.

68. This is not to say that the leading lights of the Renaissance

and the Enlightenment were all atheists, nor that theological concepts did not play an important role in their theories. Milbank shows that the origins of these disciplines can be explained only as theological constructions, and that the real moment of mystification occurs only when theology drops out (1990:28).

69. Kant is best known for his three critiques of reason, *The Critique of Pure Reason* (1781), *The Critique of Practical Reason* (1787), and *The Critique of Judgment* (1790).

70. For a more exhaustive "metacritique" of Kant's philosophy, see Milbank 1997a:7–35.

71. See Milbank 1990:20–23 on the differences between the Christian and Machiavellian conceptions of fate, fortune, and providence.

72. The modern notion of the human self as individual (literally 'un-divided one') is only two centuries old and was borrowed from the discipline of mathematics, where it denoted a freestanding entity. Citing the work of Wayne Booth, Clapp states that "the in-dividual was invented by a succession of Enlightenment thinkers and became, in its most extreme but perhaps also its most widespread interpretations, a view of the self as 'a single atomic isolate, bounded by the skin, its chief value residing precisely in some core of in-dividuality, of difference.' Thus it remains popular — almost second nature — to think we get at our 'true self' by peeling away social ties like the skin of an onion" (1996a:128, 239 n. 5). The embedded quotation is from Booth 1993:81.

73. See in this regard Rodney Clapp's splendid essay (1996b:18–33).

74. Giddens notes in these cases that "such lifestyle patterns may sometimes also involve the more or less deliberate rejection of more widely diffused forms of behaviour and consumption" (Giddens 1991:6).

75. Conversely, she adds, an abiding sense of call, of being summoned by something beyond one's self, is in our time profoundly countercultural (Norris 1996:41).

76. This review of recent books by child advocates Hillary Rodham Clinton and Marian Wright Edelman offers a superb analysis of the colonization of everyday life by expert systems.

77. The mistake made by those in the United States who believe that by reducing the size of the federal government they can "return control" of people's lives to local contexts is their assumption that national government is a self-contained sector of society. In fact it is but one facet of a vast technical complex that includes economic, social, and cultural elements. Like newborns who are physically linked and who share essential internal organs, government is inextricably bound together with the other components of a liberal society. Smaller federal budgets would not return control of people's lives to local communities, but only reconfigure the pattern of global interconnections to a relatively limited degree. The size and influence of the government is a symptom, not the cause, of the problem.

78. As recent articles in popular news magazines and business periodicals regularly observe, these knowledge environments are now organized around the personal computer.

79. It is important to note at this point that persons *qua* individuals are from the outset set over against and in competition with each other, thus perpetuating the ontological assumptions of late antiquity regarding the priority of violence.

80. Not coincidentally, Giddens notes that the terms "risk" and "chance" first appear in English only in the seventeenth century, at the beginning of the Enlightenment (1990:30).

81. See Asad 1993. The first religion to be so tamed was the church, but this technique is equally effective with other traditions as well.

82. I am deeply indebted to Cavanaugh 1995:403–404 for these insights.

83. There are no objective criteria for assessing which symbols are "most satisfactory." As Elshtain suggests in her book on the problems facing the liberal nation-state, "the individualism of an acquisitive commercial republic" cannot help but "engender new forms of social and political domination" (1995b:11).

84. A good example of the marketing of spirituality may be seen in Thomas Moore's many volumes. See, for example, 1992. For superb theological critiques of this peculiarly modern sense of spirituality, see Jones 1995, especially chapter 2, and Kenneson 1993:319–48.

85. Philip J. Lee (1987) was perhaps the first to point out the parallels between various aspects of American Protestantism and ancient Gnosticism. As I write these words television and newspapers are filled with reports of the mass suicide of a group that called itself Higher Source, in Rancho Santa Fe, California. According to news reports, the members of this group believed that they originally came from "the Level Above Human in distant space," and sought to free themselves from the bodies that they wore to accomplish their earthly task so that they could "return to the world from whence we came" (Scott Lindlaw, Associated Press, *Waco Tribune-Herald*, Friday, March 28, 1997, section A). My point is not that this group is somehow typical of contemporary American religion, but rather that only in a highly gnosticized culture could such lunacy gain currency.

86. Another splendid example of a liberal nation-state pursuing legitimate goods that anticipate the city of God is the work of the South African Truth and Reconciliation Commission. The purpose of this group, created to help shape the political culture in this fragmented country, is threefold: to provide full public disclosure of human rights violations committed during the years of the apartheid regime, consider appeals for amnesty, and recommend reparative measures. Jean Bethke Elshtain notes that "full reparation and compensation is never possible. But a political form of forgiveness as an alternative form of justice has implications that go well beyond the TRC and present-day South Africa. The TRC commissioners hope to bestow on future generations, in their own society and beyond, a vision of justice that challenges many of the models of justice with which we have long been familiar" (1997:12).

Chapter 5: Madness, Truth, and Diaspora

87. To his credit, Rorty does not reach this conclusion lightly, but "only after extensive attempts at an exchange of political views have made us realize that we are not going to get anywhere" (Rorty 1988:269).

88. It is significant to note that these powerful nations have disappeared from the political landscape, but the Jewish people continue to exist. Perhaps, as Karl Barth notes in his lectures delivered in Bonn immediately following the Second World War, the survival of

the Jewish people is the single best argument for the existence of God (Barth 1959:75).

89. I allude here to the title of a fascinating book by William H. Poteat, *Recovering the Ground: Critical Exercises in Recollection* (1994). I owe a great debt to Professor Poteat for what follows, though he is absolved from any errors and misstatements contained therein.

90. See Tanner 1988:89. The paradigmatic instance of the contrastive juxtaposition of the universal and the particular is, of course, Gotthold Lessing's well-known image of the "ugly, broad ditch" that supposedly separates the accidental truths of history and the necessary truths of reason.

91. As McClendon notes, the New Testament term *parousia* is a technical term for the official visit of a ruler within his own kingdom (1994:82).

92. According to Wright, "the early Christian kingdom-language shared the theological lineaments of the Jewish usage. Yet, even at a surface reading, this early Christian kingdom-language has little or nothing to do with the vindication of ethnic Israel, the overthrow of Roman rule in Palestine, the building of a new Temple on Mount Zion, the establishment of Torah-observance, or the nations flocking to Mount Zion to be judged and/or to be educated in the knowledge of YHWH. A major redefinition has taken place" (Wright 1997:219). The idea of a new key is taken from Robert McAfee Brown's introduction to Latin American liberation theology (1978).

93. See also the excellent piece by David F. Ford (1985:232–54).

94. And paradoxically, Boyarin adds, "the possession of territory may have made Diaspora Jewishness impossible" (1994:245). Boyarin here touches upon a problem with which Christianity has struggled since the fourth century, namely, that in the name of the God whose sovereignty over creation is manifested in Christ, Christians must rule.

95. Milbank thus observes in connection with the theological politics of St. Augustine that "the city of God is in fact a paradox, 'a nomad city' (one might say) for it does not have a site, or walls or gates. . . . Space is revolutionized: it can no longer be defended" (1990:392).

96. As many have pointed out, so long as the Romans occupied Israel the Jews continued in exile even in their own land. Boyarin, for example, observes that "the Rabbis in Diaspora in their own land also produced a phenomenon of renewal of Jewish traditional culture at the same time that they were very well acquainted indeed and an integral part of the circumambient late-antique culture" (Boyarin 1994:243; cf. Wright 1992b:268–72).

97. According to Rowan Williams, the imagery of the Eucharist "always and necessarily operates between the two poles of Maundy Thursday and Easter Sunday, between Gethsemane and Emmaus, between the Upper Room before the crucifixion and the Upper Room to which the risen Jesus comes." Our participation in the life of God in the world takes concrete form in the interval embodied in the eucharistic feast, signifying the restoration of a fellowship broken time and again by human infidelity. As a consequence, says Williams, "the wounded body and the shed blood are inescapably present" (1984:40).

98. In "Judaism as the Original Peace Church," Yoder (1985) notes that one sees in the Jewishness of Jesus and the early church the continued primacy of *Halakah*, moral reasoning about specific behavior in concrete cases, over *Haggadah*, the explication of the way the world is under the providential activity of God that makes this mode of conduct intelligible. Hence such imperatives as "go the second mile," "first be reconciled with your brother or sister," "whoever divorces his wife, except on the ground of unchastity, causes her to commit adultery, and whoever marries a divorced woman commits adultery," and "You cannot serve God and wealth" form the theoretical standpoint for interpreting events in the world.

99. Survival and service are not antitheses, but are intimately connected. Unless the church survives as a people with its own distinctive identity, it cannot render any kind of useful service to the world.

100. See Bria 1986:38–46. The drama of creation and redemption must be celebrated in both sign and deed, and both are the *leitourgia,* the public work of God's people.

101. I am indebted to McClendon for bringing Wilmore's book to my attention.

102. De Certeau rightly concludes: "Political, economic, and scientific rationality has been constructed on this strategic model" (de Certeau 1984:xix).

103. As I noted previously, the charge that is often leveled against this ecclesiology, that it advocates sectarian withdrawal from the world, is absurd.

104. Elliott Abrams contends that "the strategy of the American Jewish community presupposes that any expression of religious faith or association is dangerous to American Jewry" (Abrams 1997:34). According to Abrams, the "leaders" of American Jewry pursue this strategy even when it is factually wrong. In other words, only the kind of statecraft typical of the modern nation-state can preserve the Jewish people.

105. In some ways the battle waged by Jesus against these powers was a war of myths. See Myers 1988:14–21.

106. I am indebted to my mentor Frederick Herzog for this phrase.

107. It is in relation to these kinds of complex issues that Augustine's distinction between *frui* and *uti,* enjoying and using, is to be understood (*On Christian Doctrine* 1, 4, 22). When Christians make the right use of such practices and institutions, they do so out of a different faith, a different hope, and a different love from those recognized by the world. Edmund Hill rightly points out, however, that "the whole ethos of puritanical philistinism which has so long haunted the European outlook is descended — as a bastard indeed, but still descended — from Augustine's distinction between *frui* and *uti*" (Augustine 1991:284 n. 24). Hill only reiterates the complexity of the task of discernment that falls to the church.

References Cited

Abrams, Elliott. 1997. *Faith or Fear: How Jews Can Survive in a Christian America.* New York: Free Press.

Albright, William F. 1957. *From the Stone Age to Christianity: Monotheism and the Historical Process,* 2d ed. Garden City: Doubleday.

Allison, Jr., Dale C. 1985. *The End of the Ages Has Come: An Early Interpretation of the Passion and Resurrection of Jesus.* Philadelphia: Fortress Press.

Asad, Talal. 1993. *Genealogies of Religion: Discipline and Reasons of Power in Christianity and Islam.* Baltimore: Johns Hopkins University Press.

Augustine. 1991. *The Trinity.* Trans. Edmund Hill. Brooklyn: New City Press.

Barth, Karl. 1959. *Dogmatics in Outline.* Trans. G. T. Thompson. New York: Harper & Brothers.

Bauman, Zygmunt. 1993. *Postmodern Ethics.* Cambridge: Blackwell Publishers.

Baxter, Michael J. 1994. "'Overall, the First Amendment Has Been Very Good for Christianity' — Not!: A Response to Dyson's Rebuke." *DePaul Law Review* 43 (Winter):425–48.

Baynes, Norman H. 1955. "The Thought-World of East Rome." In *Byzantine Studies and Other Essays.* London: University of London. Pp. 24–46.

Beinart, Peter. 1997. "The New Games in Town." *The New Republic* 216:24 (June 16):23–26.

Beiner, Ronald. 1992. *What's the Matter with Liberalism?* Berkeley: University of California Press.

Belo, Fernando. 1981. *A Materialist Reading of the Gospel of Mark.* Trans. Matthew J. O'Connell. Maryknoll, N.Y.: Orbis Books.

Berger, Peter L. 1963. *Invitation to Sociology.* New York: Doubleday.

———. 1967. *The Sacred Canopy: Elements of a Sociological Theory of Religion.* Garden City: Doubleday.

Bloom, Harold. 1992. *The American Religion: The Emergence of the Post-Christian Nation.* New York: Simon & Schuster.

Bonhoeffer, Dietrich, 1955. *Ethics.* Ed. Eberhard Bethge. New York: Macmillan Publishing Co.

———. 1959. *The Cost of Discipleship,* Rev. ed. Trans. R. H. Fuller. New York: Macmillan Publishing Co.

———. 1971. *Letters and Papers from Prison,* Enlarged edition. Trans. R. H. Fuller, John Bowden, et al. New York: Macmillan Publishing Co.

Booth, Wayne. 1993. "Individualism and the Mystery of the Social Self." In *Freedom and Interpretation.* Ed. Barbara Johnson. New York: Basic Books.

Bosch, David J. 1991. *Transforming Mission: Paradigm Shifts in Theology of Mission.* Maryknoll, N.Y.: Orbis Books.

Bottum, J. 1994. "Christians and Postmoderns." *First Things* 40 (February).

Boyarin, Daniel. 1994. *A Radical Jew: Paul and the Politics of Identity.* Berkeley: University of California Press.

Bria, Ion, ed. 1986. *Go Forth in Peace.* Geneva: World Council of Churches.

Bright, John. 1953. *The Kingdom of God: The Biblical Concept and Its Meaning for the Church.* Nashville: Abingdon Press.

Brown, David. 1985. *The Divine Trinity.* La Salle, Ill.: Open Court Publishing Co.

Brown, Peter. 1988. *The Body and Society: Men, Women and Sexual Renunciation in Early Christianity.* New York: Columbia University Press.

Brown, Robert McAfee. 1978. *Theology in a New Key: Responding to Liberation Themes.* Philadelphia: Westminster Press.

Brueggemann, Walter. 1989. *Finally Comes the Poet: Daring Speech for Proclamation.* Minneapolis: Fortress Press.

————. 1991. "The Legitimacy of a Sectarian Hermeneutic." In *Interpretation and Obedience: From Faithful Reading to Faithful Living.* Minneapolis: Fortress Press.

Buber, Martin. 1967. *Kingship of God.* 3rd ed. Trans. Richard Scheimann. New York: Harper & Row. Reprinted 1990. Atlantic Humanities Press International.

————. 1970. *I and Thou.* Trans. Walter Kaufmann. New York: Charles Scribner's Sons.

Buckley, Michael J. 1987. *At the Origins of Modern Atheism.* New Haven: Yale University Press.

Burrell, David B. 1993. *Freedom and Creation in Three Traditions.* Notre Dame, Ind.: University of Notre Dame Press.

Cameron, Averil. 1991. *Christianity and the Rhetoric of Empire: The Development of Christian Discourse.* Berkeley: University of California Press.

Campbell, Colin. 1987. *The Romantic Ethic and the Spirit of Modern Consumerism.* Cambridge: Blackwell Publishers.

Carroll, John. 1993. *Humanism: The Rebirth and Wreck of Western Culture.* London: Fontana.

Cavanaugh, William T. 1995. "'A Fire Strong Enough to Consume the House': The Wars of Religion and the Rise of the State" *Modern Theology* 11 (October):397–420.

Clapp, Rodney. 1996a. *A Peculiar People: The Church as Culture in a Post-Christian World.* Downers Grove, Ill.: InterVarsity Press.

————. 1996b. "Why the Devil Takes Visa: A Christian Response to the Triumph of Consumerism." *Christianity Today* 40:11 (October 7):18–33.

Cochrane, Charles Norris. 1940. *Christianity and Classical Culture: A Study of Thought and Action from Augustus to Augustine.* London: Oxford University Press.

Commager, Henry Steele. 1977. *The Empire of Reason: How Europe Imagined and America Realized the Enlightenment.* Garden City: Anchor Press/Doubleday.

————. 1982. *The Empire of Reason: How Europe Imagined and America Realized the Enlightenment.* New York: Oxford University Press.

Cunningham, David S. 1991. *Faithful Persuasion: In Aid of a Rhetoric of Christian Theology*. Notre Dame, Ind.: University of Notre Dame Press.

Cushman, Philip. 1990. "Why the Self Is Empty: Toward a Historically Situated Psychology." *American Psychologist* 45 (May).

———. 1995. *Constructing the Self, Constructing America: A Cultural History of Psychotherapy*. Reading, Mass.: Addison-Wesley.

Daston, Lorraine. 1994. "Baconian Facts, Academic Civility, and the Prehistory of Objectivity." In *Rethinking Objectivity*. Ed. Allan Megill. Durham, N.C.: Duke University Press.

Dawson, David. 1995. *Literary Theory*. Minneapolis: Fortress Press.

de Certeau, Michel. 1984. *The Practice of Everyday Life*. Trans. Steven Rendall. Berkeley: University of California Press.

Descartes, René. 1968. "Discourse on Method." In *Discourse on Method and the Meditations*. Trans. F. E. Sutcliffe. New York: Penguin Books.

de Tocqueville, Alexis. 1945. *Democracy in America*. Vol. 1. Ed. Philips Bradley. New York: Vintage Books.

———. 1981. *De la Démocratie en Amérique*. Vol. 2. Paris: Garnier-Flammarion.

Elshtain, Jean Bethke. 1987. *Women and War*. Reprinted 1995. Chicago: University of Chicago Press.

———. 1995a. *Augustine and the Limits of Politics*. Notre Dame, Ind.: University of Notre Dame Press.

———. 1995b. *Democracy on Trial*. New York: Basic Books.

———. 1996. "Suffer the Little Children." *The New Republic* 214:10 (March 4).

———. 1997. "True Confessions." *The New Republic* 217:19 (November 10).

Figgis, John Neville. 1956. *Studies of Political Thought from Gerson to Grotius, 1414–1625*. Cambridge: Cambridge University Press.

Fish, Stanley. 1997. "Boutique Multiculturalism, or Why Liberals Are Incapable of Thinking about Hate Speech." *Critical Inquiry* 23 (Winter).

Flannery, Austin, ed. 1992. *Vatican Council II: The Conciliar and Post Conciliar Documents*. Rev. ed. Northport, N.Y.: Costello Publishing Co.

Florovsky, Georges. 1957. "Empire and Desert: Antinomies of Christian History." *The Greek Orthodox Theological Review* 3 (Winter).

Ford, David F. 1985. "'The Best Apologetic Is Good Systematics': A Proposal About the Place of Narrative in Christian Systematic Theology." *Anglican Theological Review* 67 (July):232–54.

Foucault, Michel. 1977. *Discipline and Punish: The Birth of the Prison.* Trans. Alan Sheridan. New York: Pantheon Books.

Freeman, Curtis. 1993. "The 'Eclipse' of Spiritual Exegesis: Biblical Interpretation from the Reformation to Modernity." *Southwestern Journal of Theology* (Summer):21–28.

———. 1997. "Can Baptist Theology Be Revisioned?" *Perspectives in Religious Studies* 24 (Fall):273–302.

Frei, Hans W. 1974. *The Eclipse of Biblical Narrative: A Study in Eighteenth- and Nineteenth-Century Hermeneutics.* New Haven: Yale University Press.

Funk, Robert W., Roy W. Hoover, and The Jesus Seminar, eds. 1993. *The Five Gospels: The Search for the Authentic Words of Jesus.* New York: Macmillan Publishing Co.

Giddens, Anthony. 1990. *The Consequences of Modernity.* Stanford: Stanford University Press.

———. 1991. *Modernity and Self-Identity: Self and Society in the Late Modern Age.* Stanford: Stanford University Press.

Gorringe, Timothy. 1996. *God's Just Vengeance: Crime, Violence and the Rhetoric of Salvation.* Cambridge: Cambridge University Press.

Gottwald, Norman K. 1979. *The Tribes of Yahweh: A Sociology of the Religion of Liberated Israel, 1250–1050 B.C.* Maryknoll, N.Y.: Orbis Books.

Grant, George. 1969. *Technology and Empire.* Toronto: Anansis.

Guroian, Vigen. 1987. *Incarnate Love: Essays in Orthodox Ethics.* Notre Dame, Ind.: University of Notre Dame Press.

———. 1994. *Ethics After Christendom: Toward an Ecclesial Christian Ethic.* Grand Rapids: Eerdmans.

Gutiérrez, Gustavo. 1993. *Las Casas: In Search of the Poor of Jesus Christ.* Trans. Robert R. Barr. Maryknoll, N.Y.: Orbis Books.

Hall, Douglas John. 1989. *Christian Theology in a North American Context*. Vol. 1. *Thinking the Faith*. Minneapolis: Fortress Press.

———. 1993. *Christian Theology in a North American Context*. Vol. 2. *Professing the Faith*. Minneapolis: Fortress Press.

Harvey, Barry. 1994. "Holy Insecurity: The Practice of Piety and the Politics of the Spirit." In *Ties That Bind: Life Together in the Baptist Vision*. Ed. Gary Furr and Curtis W. Freeman. Macon, Ga.: Smyth and Helwys Publishing.

Hauerwas, Stanley. 1988a. "A Christian Critique of Christian America." In *Christian Existence Today: Essays on Church, World, and Living in Between*. Durham, N.C.: Labyrinth Press.

———. 1988b. "The Church as God's New Language." In *Christian Existence Today: Essays on Church, World, and Living in Between*. Durham, N.C.: Labyrinth Press.

———. 1991. *After Christendom? How the Church is to Behave if Freedom, Justice, and a Christian Nation Are Bad Ideas*. Nashville: Abingdon Press.

———. 1995. "What Could It Mean for the Church to Be Christ's Body?" In *In Good Company: The Church as Polis*. Notre Dame, Ind.: University of Notre Dame Press.

Hauerwas, Stanley, and David B. Burrell. 1977. "Self-Deception and Autobiography: Reflections on Speer's *Inside the Third Reich*." In *Truthfulness and Tragedy: Further Investigations in Christian Ethics*. Ed. Stanley Hauerwas. Notre Dame, Ind.: University of Notre Dame Press.

Havel, Václav. 1987. "The Power of the Powerless." In *Living in Truth*. Ed. Jan Vladislav. London: Faber & Faber.

Hays, Richard B. 1989. *Echoes of Scripture in the Letters of Paul*. New Haven: Yale University Press.

———. 1994. "The Corrected Jesus." *First Things* 43 (May).

———. 1996. *The Moral Vision of the New Testament: Community, Cross, New Creation; A Contemporary Introduction to New Testament Ethics*. San Francisco: HarperSanFranciso.

Hobbes, Thomas. 1962. *Leviathan*. New York: Collier Books.

Hodgson, Peter C. 1994. *Winds of the Spirit: A Constructive Christian Theology*. Louisville: Westminster John Knox Press.

Hütter, Reinhard. 1994. "The Church as Public: Dogma, Practice, and the Holy Spirit." *Pro Ecclesia* 3 (Summer):352.

Jameson, Fredric. 1991. *Postmodernism, or, The Cultural Logic of Late Capitalism.* Durham, N.C.: Duke University Press.

Jennings, Willie. 1996. "Harlem on My Mind: Dietrich Bonhoeffer, Racial Reasoning, and Theological Reflection." Paper presented at the annual meeting of the American Academy of Religion, New Orleans, November 26.

Jenson, Robert. 1993. "How the World Lost Its Story." *First Things* 36 (October):20.

Jones, L. Gregory. 1995. *Embodying Forgiveness: A Theological Analysis.* Grand Rapids: Wm. B. Eerdmans Publishing Co.

Kenneson, Philip D. 1993. "Selling [Out] the Church in the Marketplace of Desire." *Modern Theology* 9 (October):319–48.

Kent, John H. S. 1982. *The End of the Line?: The Development of Christian Theology over the Last Two Centuries.* Philadelphia: Fortress Press.

Lafer, Gordon. 1993. "Universalism and Particularism in Jewish Law: Making Sense of Political Loyalties." In *Jewish Identity.* Ed. David Theo Goldberg and Michael Krausz. Philadelphia: Temple University Press.

Lash, Nicholas. 1986. *Theology on the Way to Emmaus.* London: SCM Press.

———. 1988. *Easter in Ordinary: Reflections on Human Experience and the Knowledge of God.* Charlottesville: University of Virginia Press.

Lee, Philip J. 1987. *Against the Protestant Gnostics.* New York: Oxford University Press.

Lehmann, Paul L. 1963. *Ethics in a Christian Context.* New York: Harper & Row.

Levinas, Emmanuel. 1989. "Ethics as First Philosophy." In *The Levinas Reader.* Ed. Seán Hand. Cambridge: Basil Blackwell.

Lindbeck, George A. 1971. "The Sectarian Future of the Church." In *The God Experience.* Ed. Joseph P. Whelan. New York: Paulist Press.

———. 1988. "The Church." In *Keeping the Faith.* Ed. Geoffrey Wainwright. Philadelphia: Fortress Press.

Linder, Robert D., and Richard V. Pierard. 1978. *Twilight of the Saints*. Downers Grove, Ill.: InterVarsity Press.

Lindlaw, Scott, Associated Press. 1997. *Waco Tribune-Herald*. March 28, section A.

MacIntyre, Alasdair. 1984. *After Virtue: A Study in Moral Theory*. 2d ed. Notre Dame, Ind.: University of Notre Dame Press.

———. 1988. *Whose Justice? Which Rationality?* Notre Dame, Ind.: University of Notre Dame Press.

Markham, Ian S. 1994. *Plurality and Christian Ethics*. New York: Cambridge University Press.

Markus, R. A. 1970. *Saeculum: History and Society in the Theology of St. Augustine*. Cambridge: Cambridge University Press.

———. 1990. The *End of Ancient Christianity*. Cambridge and New York: Cambridge University Press.

McCabe, Herbert. 1987. *God Matters*. London: G. Chapman.

McClendon, James William, Jr. 1994. *Systematic Theology*. Vol. 2. *Doctrine*. Nashville: Abingdon Press.

Meeks, Wayne A. 1993. *The Origins of Christian Morality: The First Two Centuries*. New Haven: Yale University Press.

Metz, Johann Baptist. 1980. *Faith in History and Society: Toward a Practical Fundamental Theology*. Trans. David Smith. New York: Seabury Press.

Meyendorff, John. 1979. *Byzantine Theology: Historical Trends and Doctrinal Themes*. 2d ed. New York: Fordham University Press.

Meyer, Ben F. 1986. *The Early Christians: Their World Mission and Self-Discovery*. Wilmington, Del: Michael Glazier.

Milbank, John. 1990. *Theology and Social Theory: Beyond Secular Reason*. Oxford: Blackwell Publishers.

———. 1995. "Can a Gift Be Given?" In *Rethinking Metaphysics*. Ed. L. Gregory Jones and Stephen E. Fowl. Oxford: Blackwell Publishers.

———. 1997a. "A Critique of the Theology of Right." In *The Word Made Strange: Theology, Language, Culture*. Cambridge: Blackwell Publishers.

———. 1997b. *The Word Made Strange: Theology, Language, Culture*. Cambridge: Blackwell Publishers.

Moore, Thomas. 1992. *Care of the Soul: A Guide for Cultivating Depth and Sacredness in Everyday Life.* New York: HarperCollins Publishers.

Morrison, Toni. 1992. *Jazz.* New York: Alfred A. Knopf.

———. 1993. *Jazz.* New York: Plume.

Mullins, E. Y. 1908. *The Axioms of Religion: A New Interpretation of the Baptist Faith.* Philadelphia: American Baptist Publication Society.

Myers, Ched. 1988. *Binding the Strong Man: A Political Reading of Mark's Story of Jesus.* Maryknoll, N.Y.: Orbis Books.

Newbigin, Lesslie. 1986. *Foolishness to the Greeks.* Grand Rapids: Eerdmans.

Nicholls, David. 1989. *Deity and Domination.* London: Routledge & Kegan Paul.

Niebuhr, H. Richard. 1943/1970. *Radical Monotheism and Western Culture, with Supplementary Essays.* New York: Harper & Row.

Niebuhr, Reinhold. 1932. *Moral Man and Immoral Society: A Study in Ethics and Politics.* New York: Charles Scribner's Sons.

Noll, Mark A. 1994. *The Scandal of the Evangelical Mind.* Grand Rapids: Eerdmans.

Norris, Kathleen. 1996. *The Cloister Walk.* New York: Riverhead Books.

O'Donovan, Oliver. 1996. *The Desire of the Nations: Rediscovering the Roots of Political Theology.* Cambridge: Cambridge University Press.

Ogden, Graham. 1987. *Qoheleth.* Sheffield: JSOT Press.

O'Neill, J. C. 1989. "The Origins of Monasticism." In *The Making of Orthodoxy: Essays in Honour of Henry Chadwick.* Ed. Rowan Williams. Cambridge: Cambridge University Press.

Percy, Walker. 1983. *Lost in the Cosmos: The Last Self-Help Book.* New York: Farrar, Straus & Giroux.

Polanyi, Michael. 1962. *Personal Knowledge: Toward a Post-Critical Philosophy.* Corrected ed. Chicago: University of Chicago Press.

Poteat, William H. 1985. *Polanyian Meditations: In Search of a Post-Critical Logic.* Durham, N.C.: Duke University Press.

———. 1994. *Recovering the Ground: Critical Exercises in Recollection.* Albany: State University of New York Press.

Pritchard, James B. 1969. *Ancient Near Eastern Texts Relating to the Old Testament*. 3rd ed. Princeton: Princeton University Press.

Rahner, Karl. 1974. *Theological Investigations*. Vol. 12. *Confrontations 2*. Trans. David Bourke. New York: Seabury Press.

―――. 1991. *Theological Investigations*. Vol. 22. *Human Society and the Church of Tomorrow*. Trans. Joseph Donceel. New York: Crossroad.

Ramsey, Paul. 1989. *Speak Up for Just War or Pacifism: A Critique of the United Methodist Bishops' Pastoral Letter "In Defense of Creation."* University Park: Pennsylvania State University Press.

Rieff, Philip. 1967. *The Triumph of the Therapeutic*. Chicago: University of Chicago Press.

Rorty, Richard, 1982. *Consequences of Pragmatism*. Minneapolis: University of Minnesota Press.

―――. 1988. "The Priority of Democracy to Philosophy." In *The Virginia Statute for Religious Freedom: Its Evolution and Consequences in American History*. Ed. Merrill D. Peterson and Robert C. Vaughan. New York and Cambridge: Cambridge University Press.

Rose, Gillian. 1996. *Mourning Becomes the Law: Philosophy and Representation*. Cambridge: Cambridge University Press.

Rouse, Joseph. 1987. *Knowledge and Power*. Ithaca: Cornell University Press.

Schmemann, Alexander. 1979. *Church, World, Mission*. Crestwood, N.Y.: St. Vladimir's Seminary Press.

Scholem, Gershom. 1971. *The Messianic Idea in Judaism*. New York: Schocken Books.

Scruton, Roger. 1981. *From Descartes to Wittgenstein: A Short History of Modern Philosophy*. New York: Harper & Row.

Shenk, Wilbert R. 1995. *Write the Vision: The Church Renewed*. Valley Forge, Pa.: Trinity Press International.

Silver, James W. 1957. *Confederate Morale and Church Propaganda*. Tuscaloosa, Ala.: Confederate Publishing Co.

Skinner, Quentin. 1978. *The Foundations of Modern Political Thought*. Vol. 2. *The Age of Reformation*. London: Cambridge University Press.

Smith, Harmon L. 1995. *Where Two or Three Are Gathered: Liturgy and the Moral Life.* Cleveland: The Pilgrim Press.

Smith, H. Shelton. 1972. *In His Image, But... : Racism in Southern Religion, 1780–1910.* Durham, N.C.: Duke University Press.

Smith, Ronald Gregor. 1960. *J. G. Hamann, 1730–1788: A Study in Christian Existence, with Selections from his Writings.* New York: Harper & Brothers.

Stark, Rodney. 1996. *The Rise of Christianity: A Sociologist Reconsiders History.* Princeton: Princeton University Press.

Steinmetz, David C. 1980. "The Superiority of Pre-Critical Exegesis." *Theology Today* 37 (April):27–38.

Stern, Fritz. 1961. *The Politics of Cultural Despair: A Study in the Rise of the Germanic Ideology.* Berkeley: University of California Press.

Suetonius, *Lives of the Caesars: Nero.*

Tanner, Kathryn. 1988. *God and Creation in Christian Theology: Tyranny or Empowerment?* Oxford: Basil Blackwell.

Taylor, Charles. 1989. *Sources of the Self: The Making of Modern Identity.* Cambridge: Harvard University Press.

———. 1991. *The Ethics of Authenticity.* Cambridge: Harvard University Press.

Thurman, Howard. 1949. *Jesus and the Disinherited.* New York: Abingdon-Cokesbury Press.

Tinsley, E. J. 1960. *The Imitation of God in Christ.* Philadelphia: Westminster Press.

Toulmin, Stephen. 1972. *Human Understanding.* Princeton: Princeton University Press.

———. 1990. *Cosmopolis: The Hidden Agenda of Modernity.* Chicago: University of Chicago Press.

Various. 1997. "We Hold These Truths: A Statement of Christian Conscience and Citizenship." *First Things* 76 (October):51–54.

von Harnack, Adolf. 1957. *Das Wesen des Christentums* (translated into English as *What Is Christianity?*) Trans. Thomas Bailey Saunders. New York: Harper & Brothers.

Weber, Max. 1965. *Politics as Vocation.* Philadelphia: Fortress Press.

Westerhoff, John H. 1992. "Fashioning Christians in Our Day." In *Schooling Christians: "Holy Experiments" in American Education.*

Ed. Stanley Hauerwas and John H. Westerhoff. Grand Rapids: Eerdmans.

Wilken, Robert L. 1984. *The Christians as the Romans Saw Them.* New Haven: Yale University Press.

Williams, Rowan. 1984. *Resurrection: Interpreting the Easter Gospel.* New York: Pilgrim Press.

———. 1987. "Politics and the Soul: A Reading of the City of God." *Milltown Studies* 19/20.

———. 1989. "Postmodern Theology and the Judgment of the World." In *Postmodern Theology.* Ed. Frederic B. Burnham. San Francisco: Harper & Row.

———. 1990. *The Wound of Knowledge.* 2d ed. Boston: Cowley Publications.

———. 1995. "Between Politics and Metaphysics: Reflections in the Wake of Gillian Rose." In *Rethinking Metaphysics.* Ed. L. Gregory Jones and Stephen E. Fowl. Oxford: Blackwell Publishers.

Wilmore, Gayraud S. 1982. *Last Things First.* Philadelphia: Westminster Press.

Wink, Walter. 1986. *The Powers.* Vol. 2. *Unmasking the Powers: The Invisible Powers That Determine Human Existence.* Philadelphia: Fortress Press.

———. 1992. *The Powers.* Vol. 3. *Engaging the Powers: Discernment and Resistance in a World of Domination.* Minneapolis: Fortress Press.

Wright, N. T. 1992a. *The Climax of the Covenant.* Minneapolis: Fortress Press.

———. 1992b. *Christian Origins and the Question of God.* Vol. 1. *The New Testament and the People of God.* Minneapolis: Fortress Press.

———. 1997. *Jesus and the Victory of God.* Minneapolis: Fortress Press.

Wyschogrod, Michael. 1983. *The Body of Faith: God in the People Israel.* San Francisco: Harper & Row.

Yoder, John Howard. 1977a. *The Original Revolution: Essays on Christian Pacifism.* Scottdale, Pa.: Herald Press.

————. 1977b. "Tertium Datur: Refocusing the Jewish-Christian Schism." Paper presented at the Notre Dame Graduate Theological Union, Notre Dame, Ind., October 13.

————. 1984. *The Priestly Kingdom: Social Ethics as Gospel.* Notre Dame, Ind.: University of Notre Dame Press.

————. 1985. "Judaism as the Original Peace Church." Paper presented at the Earlham School of Religion, Richmond, Ind., April 30.

————. 1989. "Withdrawal and Diaspora: The Two Faces of Liberation." In *Freedom and Discipleship: Liberation Theology in Anabaptist Perspective.* Ed. Daniel S. Schipani. Maryknoll, N.Y.: Orbis Books.

————. 1992. *Body Politics: Five Practices of the Christian Community Before the Watching World.* Nashville: Discipleship Resources.

————. 1994a. *The Politics of Jesus: Vicit Agnus Noster.* 2d ed. Grand Rapids: Eerdmans.

————. 1994b. *The Royal Priesthood: Essays Ecclesiological and Ecumenical.* Ed. Michael G. Cartwright. Grand Rapids: Eerdmans.

Zizioulas, John D. 1993. *Being as Communion: Studies in Personhood and the Church.* Crestwood, N.Y.: St. Vladimir's Seminary Press.